101 Questions and Answers on Saints

101 QUESTIONS AND ANSWERS ON SAINTS

George P. Evans

Paulist Press
New York/Mahwah, NJ

Cover design by Cynthia Dunne

Library of Congress Cataloging-in-Publication Data

Evans, George P. (George Peter).
    101 questions and answers on saints / George P. Evans.
        p.   cm.
    ISBN-13: 978-0-8091-4442-6 (alk. paper)
    1. Christian saints. I. Title. II. Title: One hundred one questions and answers on saints. III. Title: One hundred and one questions and answers on saints.
BX2325.E93 2007
235'.2—dc22

2006029109

Published by Paulist Press
997 Macarthur Boulevard
Mahwah, New Jersey 07430

www.paulistpress.com

Printed and bound in the
United States of America

CONTENTS

THE 101 QUESTIONS AND ANSWERS

ONE: THE BASICS — SAINTS 101

THREE: CANONIZATION OF SAINTS

FOUR: MARTYRDOM

SIX: THE SAINTS IN LITURGY

ACKNOWLEDGMENTS

I am grateful to those who have helped me think about this book's contents. I have met them through classes I have studied and taught, as well as in presentations I have led. Particular thanks go to Father William Sullivan and Deacon Bobby Joe Lengerich, who have helped me by reading and reacting to some of the contents. I am also grateful to Kathleen Dolan for some crucial assistance in preparing the manuscript's draft.

I hope that after reading this book, you will have gained a deeper sense of why the saints and the honoring of them have been influential in the lives of Catholics, and of others who strive to follow Jesus Christ and experience his love.

INTRODUCTION

Scratch the surface a bit, and there seems to be considerable interest in the saints. Speaking to groups of Catholic laypeople and teaching courses on various religious topics over the years, I have noticed a remarkable interest in the saints and their function in the Church's life. When sessions on prayer or the Church, for example, get around to the saints, hands go up and questions flow. This book is an attempt to gather many of those questions together and to respond to them, sometimes drawing on fine insights offered by participants in these same sessions.

In the course of preparing this book, people have asked me about its topic. My quick reply usually has been "the saints." Many assume the book must be about particular saints. As important as that kind of book is, the intent of this one is somewhat different. Its focus is "saint-*hood*," as it lives in the whole Church.

In treating vast topics, sometimes it is best to start with introductory images, picturesque ways of considering what later should be explained in fuller terms. Here I offer three images that have been helpful for me and for others. I recommend keeping them in mind while reading the rest of the book.

The first image concerns light, and it arises from a story told of a religion teacher instructing a class of young children right in the pews of a big, dark church. The teacher was reviewing various religious concepts and asked, "Who are the saints?" One youngster's hand shot up right away, and the child soon answered, "They are the ones who let God's light in." The teacher, happy to hear that interesting response, affirmed it and elaborated: "The saints, by their openness to the light that is Christ, have allowed themselves to be filled with Christ's light, such that they reflect that light to others. Let light stand for love, wisdom, truth, and all the virtues that Christ shares with the people of God." Then the teacher asked the student, "How did you come to speak the answer so well?" Immediately the child responded, "When I come to church, there is not much I understand, but I like to look at the saints on the stained-glass windows. They let God's light into the church."

The teacher was thinking metaphorically about the saints in Christian life, the student practically about physical features in church. Both combined to communicate the message of the saints' dependence on the light of Christ and their impact on those who see and receive "light" and inspiration through the saints.

Of many possible images, light has long been paramount in conveying who the saints are and what they offer the wider Church. Light is an obviously meaningful image in the life of the Church generally. The central celebrations of Easter and Christmas both draw on light as a starting point for understanding key theological themes.

We can push that imagery further. Saints on stained-glass windows are often attired in different colors, and when the light of the sun shines upon the windows, they radiate with the outside light, ultimately from the sun. Each depicted saint, with his or her array, can remind us that it is the one light of the sun that gets colored and contoured in many different ways to make an impression on those who view them. If there is darkness outside or some block between outside light and the windows, they may be unable to convey much at all. That can be a reminder that, if the light of Christ had not touched the saints, they would not have much to teach us. But since they have indeed reflected that light well, each saint gives it splendid specificity. This happily occurs when the love and virtues of Christ get exemplified in the stories, virtues, choices, places, and times that are part of individual saints' stories.

A second helpful image may be that of a journey, conveying a sense of movement, progress, and change. Consider a journey with lots of travelers devoted both to God and to their destination of living in union with God. The Second Vatican Council (1962–65) emphasized the idea of the Church as being the people of God, gifted with the presence of God and on pilgrimage toward the fullness of God's kingdom. Jesus Christ himself revealed the kingdom of God and blazed the path that leads us all forward to life with God in heaven. For Christ, this path led through joys and trials, through relationships and struggles. His cross may have seemed like an impasse, but the journey continued through Calvary and his death, to life forever and a seat "at the right hand of the Father."

From the Middle Ages comes the prominent experience of Christians going on the particular journey of a pilgrimage. Basically, pilgrims would travel together to their goal, a religious shrine. As special as this goal was, also important was the experience of prayer and companionship along the way. We may think of Christian life as a journey that follows Christ's footsteps as on a pilgrimage. Life with God in heaven is the goal. Saints are those who are walking with us as guides and exemplars along the path on which the baptized have been empowered by Christ's Spirit to travel. The saints have gone on ahead of us—they have reached the goal—but they are still connected to us. We look to them for inspiration, example, and the help of their prayers. Though subject to temptation, ill treatment, and great suffering, all the usual "harsh bumps" along the way, Christ is the perfect and sinless traveler. The saints (save Mary), though they achieved the goal of union with God through holy living, still were not completely free from sin while on earth. Different saints in various ways have made choices that slowed the journey through their own mistakes and sins. Some saints more than others needed God to pick them up, brush them off, and put them back on the right path, so much did their selfish choices bring them down. The route to heaven has different lanes and personal approaches for each pilgrim, and each one is unique. The array of individual journeys in the one great pilgrimage can remind us of the uniqueness of each one of our journeys yet also of the common quest.

A third image that conveys who the saints are is a circle, actually a ring of people centered around a central figure. Let the one in the center be Christ and those around the ring be all who receive the redeeming love of Christ. In the ringed group is a variety of persons. Mary is in the group, preeminently there but still there as a colleague to all the rest. Heaven's saints also are with us as companions on the ring. This image gives us a sense of sharing with the saints, but never apart from the centeredness on Christ that we commonly need and possess. With Christ at the center, the closer we get to Christ, the closer we move toward one another. There is a "circulation" of gifts that can enrich all gathered. The image may serve as an alternative to that of a ladder, with Christ above, those on earth at or near the bottom, and Mary and saints as go-betweens.[1]

May the history, theology, and practice connected to these three images give you some light, progress, and centeredness on Christ, as this book considers various aspects of the saints' existence.

As these three images might provide a foundation for entering into this book, so too might a simple explanation of two legitimate approaches to God, ones that have implications for the place of the saints in religious thought and practice. The two are not mutually incompatible but complementary. Each can supply a corrective to the possibility of the extreme form of the other.

The first approach holds that God far surpasses any created being in power, beauty, and love. This view reminds us never to compromise the majesty of God. Let nothing take God's place. In Christian life, this approach has often been associated with the Protestant tradition, but not exclusively so. Many mystics and spiritual writers from various Christian and other traditions would speak this message loudly and clearly. Indeed this principle is so important that no religious people can afford to ignore it!

The second approach reminds us that, to act in the world, God has worked through, and still uses, means that show both God's unsurpassed creativity and humans' use of gifts God has given them. People, structures, teachings, religious observances, art, laws, and various other instruments in the world all can point us to God's presence and action in our midst. They in turn provide us with ways of relating to God. So do people. The Catholic and Orthodox Christian Churches have traditionally emphasized this second approach.

Applied to the saints, the first view tends toward caution against esteeming saints, or anyone, to the extent that God would be displaced, but it does not necessarily rule out respect for the saints. The second approach moves toward delighting in the saints as reflecting the greatness of God and as embodying God's own gifts, but it also takes care not to put the saints in God's high place. This second slant rejoices that the saints' holiness makes us aware of the holiness of God, and that their lives give us examples of how to be committed to God. It counts as worthwhile the search for ways to honor the saints and in so doing to acclaim the God who is their life and strength.[2]

As we begin to think about heaven's saints, it will be best to avoid extremes and instead value the good directives these two approaches or principles supply.

ONE

THE BASICS—SAINTS 101

1. When Catholics speak of a "saint," what do they mean?

The word *saint* ordinarily means a deceased person who believed deeply in Jesus Christ as Lord and who lived a holy life while on earth, and as a result dwells forever with God in heaven. The person is not necessarily famous. One who fits this description and is not publicly acknowledged or honored is among those persons who are collectively celebrated in the annual feast of All Saints on November 1. God alone knows who exactly is in this category, but we can have a sense that a deceased person we have known or heard about is among these saints and belongs in this category.

The word *saint* also means, and to many people primarily means, one of those deceased holy people who is *individually and officially recognized* by the Church as holy and in heaven. Investigating the lives and virtues of candidates for sainthood, with the resulting possibility of the pope's conferring the initial title of "blessed" and finally of "saint," is a long and involved process called canonization.

There are the thousands of officially listed saints, ones declared worthy of public honor. Each of these has, and shares with many others, a saint's day on an assigned date each year. Not all of these saints have passed through a formal canonization process, for many of them were recognized during the first millennium, when the process had not come about or when it was not much advanced. Being in the official group does not mean these saints are holier or closer to God than anyone celebrated on the feast of All Saints; it does mean that their status as saints in heaven is reliable.

2. In Catholic usage, can the term *saint* also be applied to someone other than those enjoying heavenly glory with God?

Yes, it can. Unofficially and usually without much precision, Catholics and others might speak of a person as a saint or a living saint when describing someone with qualities best defined by the speaker. Usually they mean someone still living who fits each speaker's sense of a good, holy, virtuous person.

To a far lesser extent, Catholics might use the word saints more broadly to mean all those still-living believers in Christ, whether outstanding in holiness or not, and also those who have died and are not yet enjoying the life of heaven with God. The possibility for these two usages stems from the Church's self-description as a "communion of saints," a longstanding and intriguing term found in the Apostles' Creed. Many Catholics readily understand that description to mean that the Church contains three connected groups. Employing terminology long used but now less favored in theological speech, the three groups are the "Church Triumphant," or those already in heaven; the "Church Suffering," or those in purgatory; and the "Church Militant," those still on earth. Also, other Christian churches' use of the word *saint* may have affected Catholic expression and thought, especially in the ecumenical spirit of the past few decades.

This book deals with those saints who are in heaven, be they officially recognized as such or not. Still, the connection among these and the rest of the communion of saints, both those alive and those who are deceased but are still awaiting heaven, must be affirmed right from the start.

3. You say that other Christian churches' use of the word *saint* may have affected Catholic usage. In Christianity beyond Catholicism, how is the word used?

In the Protestant tradition, the word *saints* (ordinarily in this plural form) has typically referred to living believers in Christ—Church members, all the baptized—usually without any implication about their individual degree of virtue or holiness. This broad usage has roots in Saint Paul's New Testament letters to the young churches. There he often called communities of his letter-receivers saints, never addressing them in the singular. This use of the word *saints* fell out of custom a few centuries after Paul lived and wrote, and the word came to be applied to deceased people renowned for their holiness. When in the sixteenth century Martin Luther, a Scripture scholar and admirer of Paul, founded the Christian church that bears his name, he retrieved Paul's customary usage. Nowadays, following these leads, Church discourse that refers to the living as saints tends to happen much more in the Protestant tradition than the Catholic.

Many Protestant Christians both officially and unofficially use the term as Catholics do, to refer with respect to those who have died and enjoy heavenly bliss. However, the Protestant tradition generally has given far less attention to the saints in heaven than has the Catholic, owing largely to the Protestant's strong sense of God's grace that saves through *Christ alone* and to a corresponding downplaying of human cooperation with grace.

Orthodox Christians would use the term in a way similar to most Catholics, meaning primarily those individual holy ones now in heaven, including not only those known just to God but also those titled saint by the Church. These designated individuals are assigned dates for each one's own saint's day, but for the Orthodox there is no method as developed or detailed for naming saints as the one Catholics use.

4. How many saints are there, and where do we look for the answer?

An exact number eludes us! It should, of course, because there are more saints than just the canonized and the beatified. The number of saints in heaven is known only to God.

Beyond that, we have recourse to the Roman Martyrology, the official listing of not just martyrs but all the officially acknowledged saints of the Church. These include ones recognized before the canonization process developed and, since then, those subjected to that process. Since first issued in 1585 after the Council of Trent, the Roman Martyrology has been revised 131 times, recently in 1956 and 2001, and most recently in 2004 to commemorate the fortieth anniversary of Vatican II's Constitution on the Sacred Liturgy *(Sacrosanctum Concilium)*. That document expressed the vision that led to adaptations in the Church's honoring of saints in relation to its more primary adoration of God. The most recent edition of the Roman Martyrology lists approximately 6500 saints and "blesseds." "Blesseds," often canonized, have advanced through an investigatory process that grants them a degree of public honor but not the fuller veneration accorded canonized saints. This topic is discussed further in section 3. The Roman Martyrology also notes the dates for feast days. The exact number of saints cannot be enumerated, however, since many groups (like the "companions" associated with and celebrated on an individual's feast day) cannot be adequately counted.

Much smaller than this grand list is the Church's liturgical calendar, which provides for celebrations of just a few hundred saints. These are, for the most part, the better-known ones.

5. Where does the word *saint* come from, in its root meaning? To which other words is it related?

Saint means "holy person." It comes from the Latin noun and adjective with masculine and feminine versions: *sanctus/ sancta*. In Spanish, we know the masculine *san* (as in San Francisco) and the feminine *santa* (as in Santa Rosa). The Latin neuter *sanctum* means "holy *thing*." The other languages derived largely from Latin use these or closely similar words to provide this esteemed title. In English, the word appears as the noun *saint*, as the adjective *saintly* (synonymous with *holy*), and as the title *saint* (e.g., Saint Joseph). A closely related English term is *sanctity*, with its synonym *holiness*. In other languages without

English's tendency to have more than one word for the same reality, it can be easier to see that the terms *holy one* and *saint* mean basically the same, despite not looking alike.

A related term would be *sanctify,* meaning "to make holy" or "to bless," as in *sanctifying grace* (God's life in us that makes us holy people), or *sanctification* (the process of a person's becoming holy, a process that is mainly God's doing).

This sense of "making holy" can stand some explanation. The Church holds that God sanctifies and so makes the saint, since it is God's grace that renders a person holy, despite that person's need to be open to using God-given talents and resources. One does not make oneself holy or attain the status of saint by oneself. A prayer to God that says "Make me a saint" is indeed appropriate to pray to God, the real Sanctifier.

The related and derogatory term *sanctimonious* might be defined as "holier than thou," a colloquial expression denoting a proud person who acts as if he or she is holier or morally better than others. Sometimes this word's meaning, unfortunately, gets extended to describe saints. In fact, true saints are far from sanctimonious.

The Greek language uses the word *hagios* for "holy person," and that is the root for the English words *hagiology* (the study of the saints) and *hagiography* (the writings about the saints, and also the study of those writings. Hagiography is more fully examined in section 5).

6. What does *sanctity* ("holiness") mean for Christians and for the saints?

An intriguing term, *sanctity* applies, first of all, to God. Our holy God is outstanding in love, power, knowledge, beauty, and all good things. At its root, *sanctity* means "set apart," and God is surely set apart from us and all creation; God is unsurpassed and unique. This distinctiveness is God's very essence.

Christians emphasize that God, so different from us, is *love*.
God, first of all, made us to enjoy human existence. Further,
becoming one of us in Jesus Christ and sending to us the Holy
Spirit, God shares divine life with us. So, the same God who is
beyond us (is transcendent) is also close to us (is immanent).
Theologians point to a healthy tension between God's transcen-
dence and God's immanence. The very things that make God so
special and different from us—divine life and love—the Creator
God amazingly shares with creatures. So, *holiness,* a word that
fundamentally points to God's difference from us, comes also to
mean that God's own attributes are to be found in creatures of that
same God. Our holy God makes *us* holy.

Love is central to who God is, to God's holiness, and to our
own. In baptism, we have been made holy. This has happened by
God's totally free gift. It can be accepted deeply by us, and it can
be lived out through the choices and specifics of our lives.

When we try to see holiness in Christians, we look for ways
Christians reflect God's greatness. More specifically, we notice
the ways they are like Jesus Christ, who shows us God's life.
When we see a person notably embodying some of God's attributes, we might say that person is "holy"—to the extent that God's
own love motivates his or her use of those gifts. While *only* God
can determine the extent of anyone's holiness, the rest of us cannot help but sense the presence of holiness. Mother Teresa, for
example, certainly was quite widely acclaimed as holy long
before her death.

Christian holiness, then, is a very rich concept. To take a
crack at defining it, we can say that it is the presence in a person
of the free gift of God's own love and other godly traits, as these
become deeply part of someone. Christian holiness or sanctity
gives evidence of closeness to God. In a person we call holy, that
person remains human, of course, but notably bears the wonder-
ful characteristics of God. In a saint, that holiness reaches a high
level, often called "heroic virtue."

7. What does the Bible teach about holiness?

In the Old Testament, the Israelites acknowledge their Creator God as totally Other, unequalled in majesty. Isaiah proclaims: "Holy, holy, holy is the LORD of hosts" (Isa 6:3). Yet the Israelites rejoice that this God has made a covenant of love with them (Exod 20:4–6), even though they are sinners. Israel becomes a "holy nation," set apart and bound to God, after Moses meets God on Mount Sinai, a place itself called holy (Exod 19:6). Locations where God encounters and offers saving help to people end up specially dedicated to God and worthy of deep respect (e.g., Gen 28:10–22). Animals used for worship need to be pure or clean. Objects, vestments, and people dedicated to God's service in rituals get separated from the profane; that is, what is of the world, what is not necessarily bad but to be set apart from the holy. The many prescriptions insuring this "ritual purity" and covering many details of life are themselves considered holy. Being holy entails not only keeping Sabbath and adhering to rituals but also meeting God's demands for moral living. In fact, prescriptions for purity in rituals are meant to safeguard and engender moral holiness. By God's own decree to Moses, the nation of Israel is to be holy in a moral sense because its God is holy (Lev 19:2). The people are expected to hold to practices that reflect God's concerns. These practices include, for example, caring for the poor by leaving some grain in the field after harvesting, not taking revenge, honoring parents, and being attuned to the needs of those with disabilities (Lev 19:9–10, 14, 17–18).

The people of the Old Testament, then, consider the marks of holiness in God's creation to be found in the moral goodness of God's people and also in the purity qualifying people, animals, and objects to be fitting for worship's rituals.

New Testament writers similarly conceive of holiness, but with some notable expansions and differences. The holiness of God is scarcely mentioned but is assumed. It extends to Jesus, who appears as the holiness of God incarnate, "the holy one of God" (Mark 1:24). The moral imperative continues with us, as Jesus said, "Be perfect, therefore, as your heavenly Father is perfect"

(Matt 5:48); and with the message in 1 Peter 1:15: "As he who called you is holy, be holy yourselves in all your conduct."

Sanctity, however, clearly cannot be reduced to moral living. With the New Testament's revelation of Jesus Christ as God incarnate, holiness is more basically participation in God's very life. Jesus makes sure that attention to ritual purity does not stand in the way of doing the just and loving thing as people relate to God and others, especially the needy.

Christians were so conscious of God's gift of life to them and of their call to be holy that *saints* became a common term for addressing Christian communities.

8. Is holiness otherworldly?

God, the Holy One, is different from us. So, there is something transcendent about holiness. Yet, because of Christ's becoming flesh, all things human can become avenues of the holy. Holiness involves our living according to the ways of God's heaven but doing so here in our real world.

Decades ago, it was fairly common (but not correct) to think of holiness as a decidedly otherworldly reality, opposed to or barely linked with the "profane" or the "secular," or with everyday existence. In that view, our life with God has little to do with everyday relationships, tasks, decisions, and so on. In that view, sanctity encompasses merely praying, completing religious practices faithfully, obeying commandments strictly, and avoiding sin. (These are consistent with Christian holiness, as far as they go, but are incomplete.) It sometimes was said of a person who did these things, but was lacking in love or other virtues, that he or she was nonetheless holy or "a good Catholic." But this view detaches holiness from life's ordinary events and from moments when one might show kindness, enjoyment, humor, forgiveness, or understanding. Someone's holiness should never be disconnected from jobs, fears, conflicts, leisure, and similar concerns.

Teachings of the Second Vatican Council (1962–65) clearly expressed profound respect for the world, the social sciences, and the everyday experiences of our lives. Our striving for heaven, we now can say, takes us not *away* from worldly concerns but *toward* them, as we go there with Christ's mind, heart, and ways of acting. Our quest can be positively affected by our worldly involvements, nourished particularly through sacramental practice.

Holiness in an individual's life relates to "wholeness" (a sound-alike word in English that actually comes from a very different root) and to human maturity. Holiness certainly involves one's whole existence (e.g., attitudes, choices, actions, words, ideas, emotions, and relationships) wonderfully engaged in a response to the love of a saving God. If we understand wholeness as human maturity or well-balanced human living, then we have to see the link between wholeness and holiness.

In the wake of Vatican II came a welcome push toward accentuating that our progress in the following of Christ ordinarily moves in the same direction as our progress in achieving human maturity. So, growth in Christian love rightly accompanies and is helped along by factors like self-knowledge, self-acceptance, the learning of skills for respectful human interaction, and the handling of personal failures. This heightened awareness provided a breath of fresh air for many.

9. So, are holiness and wholeness just about the same?

While related, they are not the same. Some saints seemed to lack psychological wholeness or human maturity, yet they were holy. A neurotic person can still be holy, as can a developmentally disabled or mentally ill person. A person's patterns of relating to people may be limited or may need much improvement, but still that person may be holy.

William Thompson, SJ, says it well:

Holiness has to do with generosity, surrender, intensity, openness, and depth according to our capacity to possess and exercise these qualities. Holiness concerns our authenticity before God, others, ourselves, and our world, how we walk in these relationships, how we do God's will, how we remain close to God and others, how we live in harmony with God, others, and ourselves, how we cooperate with the call and grace of God in our lives....As we pass through the stages of spiritual development, we may become more psychologically mature, but whether or not we also grow in holiness depends on the quality of our response to the call of God in our lives."[3]

Psychotherapy or insights from the social sciences can be blessedly helpful in the midst of life's challenges; God can act through social sciences—as through anything—to help people toward self-acceptance, tranquility, less self-absorption, and freedom from anxiety, to name a few goals. But holiness cannot be equated with human development, personal peace, individual growth, and certainly not with worldly success or acclaim.

Indeed, true holiness never works against human maturity, even in cases where a holy person is not so whole or mature. False holiness, on the other hand, can be the enemy not only of growth toward union with God but also of development toward human maturity. Scrupulosity (sensing sin in oneself when it is truly not present, or in not accepting forgiveness once it has been given) and perfectionism (striving to be perfect in every detail of one's life) are two common examples of characteristics that can masquerade as signs of holiness but in themselves are not. Yet, even the scrupulous and the perfectionist may be holy.

10. How does holiness relate to sinfulness, failures, and deficiencies?

These realities can be springboards to growth in holiness. When I admit my own weaknesses and sins, or when I reflect on and show compassion toward others in their mistakes, I am poised to face God and rely on God's strength, forgiveness, or wisdom to guide me along. Our own failures, sinful or not, can lead us to be humble before God, patient with ourselves, and compassionate toward others; these qualities are marks of holiness.

It has often been the case that saints experience anguish, rejection, or failure for the sake of their living according to gospel values. Saints, we presume, usually committed various sins in their lives on earth, especially in their earlier years. In fact, some of them were well-known sinners for a time. It is also true that, precisely through their good response to God's love amid these trials, they experienced growth in holiness.

Holiness does *not* mean that one has never been tempted and has never sinned. Humans, save Mary, are born with original sin. Baptism gives the gift of holiness, but we have a "natural" tendency to commit sin. By the end of their lives, or after their having been purified by God's grace after their deaths, those now in heaven (canonized or not, famous or not) enjoy fullness of life with God (what is often called the "beatific vision"). We might say that their perfection is *approximately* total, with that limitation noted to differentiate their existence from the state of perfection found in God alone.

11. Can one be holy and then lose that holiness, be only somewhat holy, or be holy and sinful at the same time?

God gives the gift of holiness, the presence of God's own life in us, at baptism. The baptized one is "set apart" and made holy, and God's life is shared with that person. This action of being set apart by God through baptism happens only once in life, but it permanently characterizes the person so that it need not and cannot be repeated. The baptized are already holy in this sense, not by *their* moral choices but by God's choice to make them holy in baptism. Holiness, from this perspective, cannot be lost.

In another sense, however, holiness is not just a *gift* but a *call* given to all the baptized. It is a summons for the baptized one to respond to God's freely given help. It is a task for the baptized to choose to be and stay a holy person filled with love and with godly traits that combine with love: humility, kindness, joy, peace, patience, and other virtues. The Christian is not expected to be as holy as God is, but the Christian ought to strive to be as holy as possible in this life. In this second sense, holiness can be lost. Holiness is always "on the way" toward the goal of heroic virtue that characterizes the saints in heaven.

When we have committed a grave sin (fallen into mortal sin), we still are holy in the sense of once being set apart in baptism, but now we need to have our holiness restored in the sense of our living a life of love and virtues. That is possible, thank God, and many saints in heaven are known for their conversions from serious sin to grace.

Vatican II, particularly in chapter five of its Dogmatic Constitution on the Church *(Lumen Gentium),* teaches that all the baptized are called to holiness and to participation in church life and mission. God sounds a universal call, and there are many paths in response. The saints answer this call beautifully, in so many different eras and places, in various circumstances, through all kinds of walks of life, and with an array of personal gifts.

12. What does the phrase "the communion of saints" mean?

This has become an exciting question recently. For centuries, this affirmation in the Apostles' Creed received respect but not the depth of theological investigation given most creedal themes. Throughout the early- and mid-twentieth century, largely through its concise treatment in the *Baltimore Catechism* and similar basic books for students, the phrase came to be fairly well-known but its meaning overly simplified. It referred to those three connected parts of the Church community: in heaven, in purgatory, and on earth. The teaching usually stressed in catechesis was valid but not full enough: Those deceased who are now in heaven and live with God are called "the Church Triumphant," in the sense of sharing in Christ's victory over sin and death. The Church Triumphant can be of benefit to those on earth, who are called "the Church Militant," in the sense of still fighting against sin and evil. In turn, the Church Militant can give honor to the Triumphant in various ways. A related and emphasized teaching was that Church members both on earth and in heaven can benefit those deceased who are still being purified, who have been given the less-than-fitting title "the Church Suffering." This benefit is achieved through offering up prayers and sacrificial acts for those souls.

The phrase *communion of saints* (in Latin, *communio sanctorum*)—which is not explicitly biblical yet has scripturally based content—entered the Apostles' Creed by at least the fifth century. Without dismantling the main points known to many Catholics, recent scholars and teachers have given it new attention. *The Catechism of the Catholic Church* (#954–#962) presents a clear and rich explanation. It teaches that the phrase can be interpreted in two valid ways suggested by medieval theologians. It can mean "communion among holy things" (participation in the eucharistic body and blood; from the Latin genitive neuter plural) or "communion of holy people" (a body of people; from the genitive masculine plural). Quoting the thirteenth-century theologian St. Thomas Aquinas, the *Catechism* shows how this dual communion is centered in Christ: "All of us, however, in varying degrees and in different ways share in the same charity toward God and our neighbors, and we all sing the one hymn of glory to our God. All, indeed, who are of Christ and who have his Spirit form one Church and in Christ cleave together" (#954).

The sacramental understanding ("holy things," from the Latin *sancta*) is probably older than the more personal meaning ("holy people," from the Latin *sancti*), as theologians since the nineteenth century have advanced.

Participation in the Eucharist builds those who receive that sacrament into a holy people, sharing among one another benefits such as friendship in Christ, mutual prayer, and good example. Communion of saints means a sharing of spiritual "goods," always with Christ as the source of these good things, received by God's people and then exchanged among them. As the *Catechism* explains, these goods can include shared faith, charisms (gifts the Spirit gives to one or a few individuals for building up the wider Church), common ownership of possessions, and charitable acts.

The roots of the communion of saints lie in the great solidarity existing among the three persons of the Trinity. God's life, especially through the Holy Spirit's power and love, moves outward and wants to animate those God has created and saved. The *communio sanctorum,* then, is the extension, the product, or the reflection of the *communio Trinitatis.*

13. In our world of many different faiths, how universally applicable is the term *saint*?

Saint is a Christian term in origin and root meaning; it transfers only limitedly beyond Christianity. Looking for saints in other traditions seems to put those religious groups in the awkward position of fitting into a Christian mold. Their absence of a relation to Christ indeed constitutes a definite difference. Nevertheless, there can be found in these religious groups figures outstanding in holiness, itself a word understood in other traditions in ways both similar to and different from its Christian meaning.

Recent scholars of comparative religion frequently use the term *holy person.* It describes someone having a reputation for virtues prized in a religious tradition and also someone embodying sacred power. The historian Peter Brown coined the term in a lecture decades ago,[4] and with the help of other scholars he has refined his ideas since then.

To elaborate on the idea of the holy person, Brown and colleagues see this figure as often being possessed of various estimable traits. The sacred power embodied by the holy person may be communicated to others through wisdom in speech, through social interaction, through miracles performed while the holy person is alive, and, especially after his or her death, through the holy one's relics. The exemplary role has to do with his or her having lived morally well.

What are needed for the holy person to make an impact, beyond the person's own holiness, are ways in which the culture can respect the holy one enough to let his or her gifts be known and cherished. This happens through roles the person can fulfill, and through means the community might use to promote the holy person's story in oral and written forms.

In a qualified way, most faiths have one or a few terms for holy persons esteemed for the way their lives were lived. Judaism, out of respect for the First Commandment ("I am the Lord your God...; you shall have no other gods before me." Exod 20:2–3; Deut 5:6), has a deep-seated tendency to avoid holding up people who would be seen as exemplars of virtue or intermediaries with God. Despite this strong main thrust, some strains of Judaism have revered biblical heroes; there are also the *Hasidim,* Jewish followers of individual masters who embody the power of mystical teachings. Islam, too, has an inbuilt suspicion of honoring figures as holy. However, more than in the Jewish tradition, some groups have been widely venerated in Islam. These are teachers, ascetics, and especially martyrs. Hinduism distinguishes between holy persons and divine beings appearing in human form. Hinduism respects especially people who have had close relationships to divinities, wonderworkers who have achieved spiritual liberation through austerity, and people who are great teachers. Buddhism's holy ones are those who achieve enlightenment.

14. Is Jesus a saint? Is Mary? How do they compare to those honored as saints?

All the saints, being not divine but human, lived as real people in need of being redeemed. Jesus Christ is not only human but is the very God who has redeemed humanity. The word *saint* does not apply to him, the only human who is the agent and not a recipient of redemption. Jesus Christ is thus not given the title, although he has the fullness of holiness.

Saints do not lose their humanity, even though they evidence heroic virtue and become fine examples of those who have become "like unto God." They never become God or become angels.

Mary, a human person and thus in need of redemption, received it not through baptism (as have other humans) but through her being preserved from original sin in her immaculate conception. Mary, *unlike* Christ, is indeed a saint, but she is unique among the saints. Of all humanity, only Mary is Mother of God. Only she is ever-sinless among the whole varied company of saints.

In the Church's early centuries, a very helpful distinction was proposed, widely promoted, and finally set in place as official Church teaching at the Second Council of Nicaea in 787. It differentiated between *latreia,* the adoration owed only to God (Father, Son, and Spirit), and *dulia,* the veneration offered to the saints. For Mary, the honor paid her is termed *hyperdulia,* an intensified form of veneration offered only to her. In fact, Mary has been called, according to one of her many titles, Queen of All Saints.

The phrase "Mary and the saints" is frequently used but it can be misunderstood. It should *not* imply that Mary is not a saint but rather that she is one who is quite different from the rest. Recent decades have seen Mary prized, not only as unique among humans and even saints, but also as exemplary, as the first of the redeemed, one who is a model of the faith, courage, and love that all Christians are called to muster.

15. Since the saints are a "varied company," are there groupings or categories of saints in the Church's life and prayer?

Saints have been grouped in various ways. First of all, there are the titles used in liturgical celebrations. The Church has set these categories, and saints are included under them as they fit criteria. The last revision of the categories was but a slight one, made soon after Vatican Council II.

There are four so-called traditional titles: *apostle* (the Twelve, plus Paul and Barnabas), evangelist (a Gospel author), *martyr* (a Christian who suffered death for faith in Christ), and *virgin* (never-married women, not men, of consecrated life). Then there are the titles for various clergy, with the same ones employed for diocesan or religious: *pope, bishop, priest,* and *deacon.* There is also the eminent title *doctor of the Church* of which there are only thirty-three. (The term is explained more fully in the next response.) Titles related to religious orders are these: *abbot* (leader of a monastery), *hermit* (a solitary living a consecrated monastic life), *monk* (male who has taken solemn vows), and *religious* (here meaning nonordained male in simple vows, or a woman who was married before her religious consecration). Many saints belong under more than one title (e.g., virgin and martyr). A few saints have no title, but that does not place them in a lower status at all.

Some commentators have suggested that a few new titles are needed, ones more in keeping with the pastoral roles of the Church today. Possible titles for future revisions might include roles carried out by laity. So, someday it might be possible to honor saints under titles such as layperson, husband, wife, father, mother, prophet, teacher, to name but a few.

Aside from these official liturgical titles, other groupings can be proposed and helpfully used in catechesis, such as the following more or less prominent ones: missionary, ascetic, theologian, diplomat. Many of the recently formulated Protestant lists of exemplary figures who were suggested for remembrance in worship services feature interesting and broader categories, such as composers, prophets, and artists. Lawrence Cunningham has grouped saints and would-be saints under some classifications noted above but also these: pilgrims, warriors, mystics, humanists, activists, and outsiders.[5] This array nicely expands the rather limited official categories, and it reminds all that holiness can be lived through many paths. In the Catholic church it would be possible to expand and adapt the liturgical categories in years to come, but that would never be done in a way that ignores cherished traditional titles.

16. What exactly qualifies a saint to be called a "doctor of the Church?"

"Doctor" is used here in the sense of a teacher, scholar, or learned person. However, that alone is not enough to give one this prized designation. Three requirements must be met. First, the person must already be recognized officially as a saint of the Catholic Church. Second, he or she must indeed be judged to be learned. Third, the title must be conferred by the pope (in practice, almost always) or an ecumenical council—not by popular opinion nor by just any group or individual.

A doctor of the Church, one of a select group, must present some faith truth or truths in a relatively groundbreaking way that might be said to unlock a bit more the mysteries of God for God's people. So, a doctor is a pastorally significant saint.

Until the sixteenth century, there were just eight doctors, four each from the West and the East. From the West were Ambrose (d. 397), Augustine (d. 430), Jerome (d. ca. 420), all bishops; and Gregory the Great (d. 604), pope. They all were officially recognized as doctors in 1298. The earliest proclaimed Eastern doctors were John Chrysostom (d. 407), Basil the Great (d. 397), Gregory Nazianzus (d. ca. 390), and Athanasius (d. 373), all bishops. These saints were all recognized as doctors in 1568, along with Thomas Aquinas, Dominican monk (d. 1274). No martyrs were or have been counted among the doctors, despite some being notably learned. Martyrs deserve to be esteemed in a way all their own.

In 1588, Bonaventure, cardinal (d. 1274), was made a doctor. Over a century later, in 1720, Anselm, bishop (d. 1109) became the first of many more doctors added in the eighteenth through twentieth centuries. In 1970, the first two women were named doctors: Teresa of Avila, Carmelite religious (d. 1582), and Catherine of Siena, religious (d. 1380); Therese of Lisieux, Carmelite religious, joined them in 1997, the centenary of her death.

The number of doctors now stands at thirty-three. Among these are two popes, eighteen bishops, nine priests, and a deacon.

17. Who are probably the most admired saints?

With recourse to a few polls, with allowance for area differences and popular opinion, and excepting Mary and biblical saints, here are ten who probably rise to the top:

St. Francis of Assisi, deacon (d. 1226), is arguably the world's most beloved saint. This Italian son of nobility made himself materially poor and practiced gentleness, humility, obedience, patience, and deep respect for God's creation. In founding the Franciscans, he helped God's love and truth to be spread worldwide.

St. Thérèse of Lisieux, Carmelite (d. 1897), died at age twenty-four after a simple but hard life of blessings amid many losses. Insightful and sensitive, she prayed from her Carmelite cloister in France for the Church's mission everywhere. Her "little way," relying on Christ's strength and doing small things with extraordinary love, has inspired millions.

St. Thomas More (d. 1535), a lawyer, writer, and statesman, rose to be chancellor to British King Henry VIII. A husband and a father, he stood against his king to be faithful to his God and to do what his conscience deemed right. For this he suffered a martyr's death.

St. Teresa of Avila (d. 1582) joined Carmel in her native Spain and was drawn to deeper prayer and virtue. She drove a significant reform among Carmelites. Her struggles to live authentically, to persevere in prayer, and to relate to others teach the value of perseverance despite false starts and challenges.

St. Augustine (d. 430), a searcher for truth and love who wandered before committing to Christ, shared that journey in his *Confessions.* As monk, pastor, theologian, and bishop, he offered brilliant insights, still heeded today. He lived in Northern Africa and Italy.

St. Catherine of Siena (d. 1380), a secular Dominican in Italy, gave God her life of solitude, prayer, and charity. She bravely confronted and helped right serious problems within Church structures.

St. Patrick (d. 461) was the great missionary and bishop in Armagh, Ireland, whose gifts and teachings formed a people dedicated to Christ. Catholics from throughout the English-speaking world know at least vaguely of his zeal and deeds.

St. Francis Xavier (d. 1552), a Spaniard and a founding member of St. Ignatius Loyola's Society of Jesus, brought his conviction that Jesus Christ is the world's savior to his mostly successful but demanding missionary labors in and around India and the Far East.

St. Thomas Aquinas (d. 1274), an early Dominican friar from Italy, drew upon the treasures of the Church's tradition, the riches of philosophical discourse, and the depths of his own intelligence and prayer to give the world his magnificent theological and devotional texts.

St. Anthony of Padua (d. 1231) was a Portuguese-born early Franciscan who served in Italy for years. He preached to refute heretics and served as professor of theology. He is famous as patron of those needing to find lost items.

Who would you *add to this list, and why?*

18. Is there more than just a close chronological link between the celebrations of Halloween and All Saints' Day, and how did that religious observance begin?

Many people do not realize that Halloween and All Saints' Day are related. Lots of people who celebrate the secular observance of Halloween do not even know there is an All Saints' Day or know what it is. In fact, the two are related, even though they have now "grown apart."

Halloween, October 31, has its own significance. In some places, a festival of the dead deriving from the Druids had been associated with the end of harvest. The Druids held that November 1, coming at a time after the harvest was gathered and being in a season of diminished light of day, marked the start of a new year. October 31 was held to be a night when the souls of all who died in the previous year went to the next world. To assist these dead on their way, sacrifices to the gods were offered, and bonfires were kindled to light up the sky. In addition, in popular lore fairies, witches, and goblins were thought to destroy crops and kidnap children on this night. When the celebration of All Saints' Day was moved to November 1 (more on this below), the celebration of its eve received a Christian slant. At least in some places children dressed as saints, and people prayed to saints. In England, the night came to be known as All Hallows Even (Evening) or Halloween. But the pagan traditions, though adapted and usually softened, have stayed with the observance of the eve. In the last few decades, at least in North America, Halloween has become more and more prominent and secular. Many Christian communities, trying to shift this emphasis back to its roots, have begun to encourage children to dress in imitation of their patron saints on or near All Saints' Day, a feast with its own interesting history.

Before the widespread martyrdom of Christians ended, there were harsh persecutions that resulted in a strong consciousness of the martyrs' ultimate sacrifice. Thus, by the early fourth century, the number of individual martyrs' feast days increased greatly. In that climate rose a liturgical feast devoted to all the martyrs, so that those without particular feasts might still be honored. In the Church of Eastern Europe and nearby parts of Asia, the celebration began on Friday in Easter week. We cannot be sure why this specific timing emerged. Perhaps it was to allow Easter's newly baptized a chance to focus on the martyrs' strong commitment to their baptism. Whatever the reason, that day gave way after many decades to another, the first Sunday after Pentecost (when Eastern Rite Catholics and the Orthodox still honor all saints). In Rome and the West, a similar celebration took hold only in the early seventh century. That is when Rome's Pantheon temple building was converted to Christian use. It was dedicated as the Church of St. Mary and All the Martyrs on May 13 in 609. This date became Rome's annual day for feting, not all saints, but all martyrs.

19. How did the celebration of All Saints' Day broaden from celebrating all martyrs to honoring all saints, and get moved to November 1? What is its focus now?

As decades and centuries moved along, the number of added celebrations of saints—after the fourth century, mostly nonmartyrs—grew steadily. By the eighth century the Church at Rome had broadened the observance of all the martyrs to encompass "all saints." Historical data is hard to piece together concerning the feast and especially the reasons for its transfer in the West to November 1. In England, Ireland, and Germany, that move probably had happened by the start of the ninth century. That would have made sense, so that abundant feasting could be assured after the harvest was completed. The switch may have been made first in one of these places, or it may have spread from Rome, where a chapel honoring the many categories of saints was built at St. Peter's in the mid-eighth century. In any event, celebrating on the first of November expanded to all the West, and it has held fast.

With the growing prominence of the doctrine of purgatory in the Middle Ages came prayers for those deceased who would be in purgatory before their eventual entrance into heaven. Around the year 1000, an abbot at Cluny in France began observing November 2 as a day to pray for the dead. All Souls' Day caught on and spread. In a way, its timing may diminish the impact of All Saints' Day and the message that many are already enjoying the victory of God's grace in heaven. In another way, the two celebrations are complementary, as they point us toward those already in heaven and those still being cleansed for entrance there.

All Saints' Day's location near the end of the liturgical year helps us consider the saints as having reached the goal of all Christians: life of perfected holiness in the fullness of the kingdom with God. The Mass of All Saints' Day features, for its first reading, a description of the heavenly Jerusalem from Revelation, chapter 6, and, in the second reading, 1 John's reminder that our already being adopted children of God is the foundation of our future glory. The Gospel is a proclamation of the Beatitudes as outstanding characteristics of holy people.

While All Saints' Day indeed points toward *every* saint, even those with their own days of memorial in the calendar, in a special way it is for the many more known only to God to be already enjoying heavenly bliss. These "splendid nobodies," as Elizabeth Johnson has termed them, can thus give hope and joy to us on the way.[6]

20. Do the saints know our thoughts?

This question is a good example of speculative theology. Indeed, what could be more speculative than questions of life beyond death! While we need to beware of any overly easy answers about details of the life of those in heaven, neither are we without insights. Not all theological matters are definitively settled, and this issue is in that category.

The most accepted theological opinion in Catholic circles seems to say that, on their own, the saints in heaven do *not* have universal access to our ideas. Humans, as we well know, do not have God's capacity for knowledge. The saints are human still, unlike heaven's angels. Moreover, with the exception of perhaps just Mary (assumed body and soul into heaven), the saints are in an intermediate state; they have died but they have not yet experienced the reuniting of soul and body. By themselves, they do not perceive what those with bodies can grasp. By virtue of God's granting them the "beatific vision," the blessedness of intimate sharing with God, they gain their knowledge directly from God. God can, and we presume does, make saints aware of requests for their intercession. While theirs is not God's full knowledge, still it is a loving knowledge freed from limitations and biases of earthly knowing and relating.

21. The connection between saints and angels is intriguing. Some angels are listed among the saints. And sometimes people refer to those who have died, especially children, as angels. Is this reference official Catholic belief, and are saints actually quite similar to angels?

In a word, no. Those references are inexact or poetic attempts to describe the deceased's closeness to God and their freedom from the confines of earthly or bodily suffering. These are states natural to angels.

In fact, saints and angels are quite different. The saints, except Mary (assumed body and soul into heaven at her glorious assumption), await God's action of reuniting their spirits with their bodies in the resurrection of the dead. Their existence now as temporary bodiless spirits reminds us of the angels' *permanent* existence as such, but it does not change the fact that the saints are humans, *not* angels.

Although both angels and humans are personal beings created by God, each is a different "order" of beings. Humans are both physical and spiritual, but angels are only spiritual. Humans *have* spirits (i.e., have a spiritual dimension to their beings), but angels *are* spirits. Even after death, the basic nature of a human does not change. When the spirit leaves the body at death, it is without what it needs to be complete. From death until the resurrection of the body, that human spirit lives in anticipation of being reunited with its body. An angel, on the other hand, is a spirit that forever lives without a body.

Angel literally means "messenger." In terms of what they do, angels are most often described as servants and heralds of God, roles not foreign to humans and certainly not to saints. As the story of the fallen angel Lucifer shows, angels are like humans in having intelligence and will. Both angels and saints live in heavenly bliss with God. These similarities between angels and humans make it not so surprising that some mixing of ideas about angels and saints has occurred.

In a colloquial way, someone might also refer to another human person as "an angel" in the sense that the person is good, spiritually strong, kind, generous, and so on. These qualities, of course, can be marks of holiness befitting a saint. Since angels are pure spirits, this usage might be considered a complimentary though inexact description of how the spiritual dimension of that particular human person is so well developed.

Indeed some angels are counted and celebrated among the saints, but the term *saint* applies to an angel only in a stretched sense of sainthood. Over the centuries, the whole group of guardian angels and a few archangels came to be listed among the catalogued saints. This is probably because grassroots devotion to them emerged and developed a momentum, often spurred by particular events. For instance, St. Michael the Archangel's fifth-century apparition in Italy led to the building of a shrine, around which veneration of Michael grew. In the Bible, the archangels took on a seemingly human form to carry out their roles as God's messengers. Unlike other angels but like some saints, they are called by name in Scripture and now can be invoked by name for their prayers to God. Doing such important work for God, their holiness has been presumed.

Archangels Gabriel, Michael, and Raphael, mentioned by name in the Bible and once remembered on separate days, now share a memorial in the calendar on September 29. Guardian angels are liturgically remembered on October 2.

Two

Honoring the Saints, Past and Present

22. In which ways are saints typically honored in Christian life?

The kinds of honor given the saints can be considered simply under four basic categories. In these ways and within the communion of saints centered around Christ, saints' devotees both acclaim the saints and hope to receive various benefits from them.

Remembrance of the saints is fundamental. This remembrance happens frequently through story, public prayer, and private devotion to the saints, a "cloud of witnesses" (Heb 12:1). Formal investigation of stories about, and virtues of, sainthood candidates yields the whole Church a reliable list (a "canon") of saints. "Canonized" saints offer assurance that some deceased have attained glory with God. Our remembering them reinforces their link with us in the communion of saints. By recalling the experiences, qualities, and struggles that were theirs on earth, as well as their glorious life now in heaven, we are strengthened to commit ourselves to the same God they have known, loved, and served. Their witness can inspire hope, courage, faithfulness, and joy.

Similarly, veneration of saints can happen in many ways. For example, people name children and churches after saints, cherish relics, and install depictions of them (pictures, statues, icons) in places of honor in churches and homes. Saints ordinarily are venerated for reaching a level of holiness that their devotees have not attained. Nevertheless, this veneration is usually more wholehearted and enthusiastic when devotees sense some link or similarity between themselves and a saint.

Imitation or emulation of saints is not an aping of the externals of their lives, like choice of clothing or the like, but rather a reflective consideration of—and a quest to make our own—a saint's attitudes, values, convictions, and works. For imitation to be possible, people ordinarily need to have proper knowledge of a saint, usually through good biographical information and sometimes through the saints' writings. Saints whose stories are naturally interesting, well told, and relevant to hearers are in a good position to be imitated.

Invocation (from the Latin *vocare,* "to call") of the saints is the practice of praying to one or more of them, but not as the ends in the line of prayer. For what result do devotees of saints pray to them? People customarily pray to the saints that the saints might in turn intercede for their petitioners; that is, might pray for their needs before God. Sometimes, however, people have prayed to the saints for their direct aid. Of these four features—remembrance, veneration, emulation, and invocation—invocation indeed has been the most controversial one in the history of Christian belief and practice.

23. What, in brief, has been the history of honoring the saints in the devotion and life of the Church?

Christians believed in the resurrection of Christ, and they prayed with and for one another and for their dead to God through Christ's intercession. To their community's early martyrs, who died bravely on account of their faith in Christ, they ascribed quick entry into a place with Christ in heaven. They prized the martyrs' bodily remains and commemorated their anniversaries of death with eucharistic celebration at their tombs, thus linking Christ's sacrifice on Calvary with the martyrs' self-sacrifice. They soon began praying, not *for* martyrs, but *to* and *through* martyrs for their intercession with Christ. The martyrs, all lauded as saints after they died, came to represent the ideal of holiness. The stories of their deaths and the events leading to them were told and cherished.

In and after the fourth century, when persecutions ended and Christianity became the official religion, honoring martyrs expanded to include other holy deceased whose lives were exemplary: virgins, ascetics, and monks as well as bishops and remembered New Testament figures—and also, more and more, Mary. Saints' bodies frequently were moved, and their relics (body parts and personal objects) were often transferred to new locations for honoring. Shrines were built at these new locations, attracting people's widespread devotion, especially through pilgrimages. The honoring of saints became very strong in Christian piety. With a firm belief that miracles could happen through saints' intercessory prayers or their powers, people passed down their favorite, often-embellished stories of saints, and of their miracles and feats, both in life and in death.

In time, more sophisticated and authoritative procedures for classifying certain esteemed figures as saints were needed, with approvals by local bishops eventually giving way to the prerogative of the pope to canonize, or definitively list saints in the canon, after investigation. At its best, the tradition saw the saints within the "Body of Christ" as friends of Christ, their savior and intercessor, and heavenly friends or companions of those on earth. At its worst, the tradition was a tendency toward superstitious exaltation of saints to the position of mini-deities, despite attempts to curb this behavior. This happened amid criticisms lodged by some heretical groups but also by some faithful Christians. As the late Middle Ages unfolded, the "cult (honoring) of the saints" grew ever stronger. Fairly often voiced was a particularly troublesome concern that saints were treated as having attributes actually belonging only to God.

At the Reformation, controversies over honoring the saints came to a head, and the place of the saints in the Church faced upheaval. By then, devotion to the saints had become a hallmark of Christian religious life. The sixteenth century's Protestant Reformers reacted against long-established ways of honoring the saints—as did some Catholics too.

24. In all of this, what has been the standard way of conceiving the connection between God's people on earth and God's saints in heaven?

For centuries, this link has been described in terms of human relationships drawn from the secular world. The most prominent way of expressing the bond has been the patron-client model, derived from the ways of ancient Roman society. It has been strong since the fourth century, though in many places less so in the recent past. It came in for strong rejection in the Protestant Reformation. While it holds on still, the Second Vatican Council offered the makings of a richer way of expressing the link.

In the earthly patronage system, people sought to obtain favors or advance "up the ladder" in their fields of work. They asked for and received assistance from those already established. The more advanced persons would typically "put in a good word" or offer direct help on behalf of those looking for their favor.

In the feudal system that flourished in Europe in the High Middle Ages (900–1300), the patron-client system got transposed to a heavenly sphere, wherein God reigns supreme at a distance. In this view, the saints, as "friends in high places," intercede with God and offer direct help, and those on earth pray to them and offer them honor. All this happens within the communion of saints.

This system stresses the working of wonders or miracles through the saints' position and power. God's own presence and power comes close to people by means of the saints as God's channels, instruments, or go-betweens. People ask for help of both material and spiritual kinds through and from the saints, and then give prayerful thanks for favors received.

It should be noted that the array of devotions to saints flourished in the midst of a strong sense of sinfulness among God's people on earth. With that came the corresponding notion that they are few in number who will be saved and go to heaven. Both ideas were hallmarks of religious thought in the Middle Ages. People were conscious of their need for spiritual assistance, but many were not able to grasp the deep content of theology, the sophistication of the Church's best prayers and hymns, or the cautions against super-stition spoken by Church leaders.

25. What is the origin of the controversial practice of the invocation of saints?

The invocation of saints arose in the earliest Christian centuries out of a strong sense that all those who are closely joined in the Body of Christ can pray for one another to and with Christ, who is the unequaled redeemer and intercessor (1 Tim 2:4). Trusting in the power of Christ and the Spirit to hear and answer their prayers, the earliest Christians customarily prayed for one another. They also asked one another to pray to God for themselves. When martyrs died, Christians began praying *to* them – began asking for their prayers—with a trust that those deceased were still participants in the intercession Christ performs. They no longer prayed *for* the martyrs since they were widely held to be already enjoying fullness of life with God. At first, these prayers to the martyrs were offered as acts of private devotion, and later some prayers to saints became a part of the liturgy. So, invocation, then as now, rested on a firm trust that the saints can and do intercede with God for those who ask their prayers.

With the emergence of the patron-client model for Christians' understanding of their link to the saints, invocation of the saints became more and more a dominant way to honor them. Petitioners regularly prayed to one or more saints with the sense that the saints in turn would pray to God for petitioners' needs; sometimes the prayers to the saints were for direct aid that the petitioners trusted those saints could and would provide.

Prayers to the saints, especially patron saints, became one of the foremost features of Christian spirituality in the Middle Ages. The reformer Martin Luther counted himself among those who prayed to the saints faithfully, until he began to look at things quite differently.

26. Is the custom of people having patron saints related to this patronage system?

Yes. The still-strong practice of connecting a particular canonized saint in an assisting way to a specific living person, group, need, or cause is indeed related to the view of the saints in general as figures in a patron-client relationship. Patron saints are counted on to provide a sense of rather particular accompaniment along the Christian journey, primarily through example and prayers. In turn, their devoted individuals or groups honor them, often by praying to them or studying and promoting their life stories and writings.

Although rooted in the Roman system of patronage, the practice of picking or receiving a patron saint is not surprising to find in the Catholic tradition, given the strong historical place of a sense of companionship that exists among all who live in the Body of Christ. It makes sense that a follower of Christ would want to honor not just the saints in general but also particular ones. Angels came to be perceived also as patrons; this seems fitting since they are considered God's messengers to persons in crucial moments.

The word *protector,* often used to describe the help each patron saint offers, can be tricky to use, if protection suggests the patron's substitution for or equality with the all-providing God.

As awareness of saints as intercessors developed, people of particular towns, occupations, hobbies, and situations in life naturally looked to individual saints to inspire them and to receive their prayers for needs of all kinds. This custom gradually grew, with people often selecting personal patrons because of their own interest in and respect for some features of the lives of those saints.

Christians started to bear names of saints at least by the fourth century, and people often thought of the saints whose names they bore as their patrons. Churches and other religious institutions began to be named for saints too. (See section 8.)

Saints often ended up as patrons of places and churches because those saints' relics were located there. On sites of saints' tombs, churches often would be built; these would routinely take these saints' names. Over time, these same saints often became revered patrons of the residents of the towns.

In the Middle Ages, "confraternities" or brotherhoods were formed and often dedicated in part to spreading devotion to individual patron saints. These groups provided gatherings for prayer, companionship, and charitable deeds, as well as for keeping alive the notoriety of the patron saint. A confraternity often displayed and honored relics of its patron saint.

27. How do patron saints get designated?

The connection between patron saints and individual devotees can be forged by personal selection ("I admire the story of St. Joan," or "I trust that St. Jerome intercedes for me."). Or, it can happen first by the Church's designation, then made personally meaningful by the devotee's choice. ("I am a dentist, and St. Apollonia is listed officially as patron of my profession; I pray to her.")

Individuals are free to select personal patron saints unofficially for any good reason. There are various published lists of patrons and the corresponding profession, activity, locale, or cause associated with each saint. Most listed matchups (particularly centuries-old ones) developed from the grassroots experiences of people wanting to be close to saints, and others (especially more recently entrusted ones) were officially devised by the Holy See of Rome. Not every saint is a designated patron. In general, proposed patronages for churches or groups must be approved by the local bishops or the Holy See.

Usually there is some facet of the saint's life that connects more or less clearly with the designated group, place, or activity. For example, it is logical that St. Joseph, foster-father of Jesus Christ, received patronage of the whole Church, the Body of Christ. However, some saints are entrusted with causes that can keep many wondering how the connection came about. St. Clare of Assisi is the patron saint of television. A story about her tells that, when she was ill and confined to her room, she saw and heard the Mass nonetheless there at a distance from where it was being celebrated. So Pope Pius XII placed the new invention of television, a visual and aural medium, under her care!

In many cases, the saint lived in a place, held a job, or experienced a challenge of which he or she is now patron. For example, St. Francis Xavier, the renowned sixteenth-century Jesuit missionary, is copatron of missionaries. St. Francis de Sales, seventeenth-century bishop and evangelizer, has long been noted for his ministry of writing, and so not surprisingly is he patron of journalists. St. Thérèse of Lisieux in France has been made copatron of her homeland.

Sometimes, the connection calls for some explanation. The other copatron of missionaries is the same St. Thérèse, a nineteenth-century French Carmelite nun who only once left her own country and never was a missionary (though she longed to be one). The designation is attributable to Thérèse's gaining wide acclaim after death for her prayerful support of missionaries during her life.

At other times, the connection needs even more explanation. Here again, Therese can be the example. Because she predicted, before her impending death, that she would send a shower of roses to earth from heaven, she is considered patron of florists.

Still other saints get their patronage from the meaning of their names. The early Christian martyr and virgin Lucy is patron of sufferers of eye ailments, and this stems from her name's derivation from the Latin word for light *(lux, lucis)*.

28. What is the background of some of the best known patronages; namely, St. Anthony for lost articles, and St. Jude for hopeless causes?

Many have prayed: "Dear St. Anthony, come around. Something's lost and can't be found." Just after the Franciscan friar Anthony of Padua's death in 1231, people began going to his tomb and praying there for many needs. The common opinion was that petitions to Anthony brought results. This reputation seems to have secured his place as intercessor. The particular connection to lost items seems rooted in legends. One tells that Anthony's valuable academic notebook was stolen. Anthony's prayers brought its return, and he showed mercy and reconciliation to the thief. Another holds that, after a young man had cut off his own limb, Anthony restored it. His patronage of lost items shows the power of medieval legends and reputations for sanctity. Anthony is patron of many other needs too. So widespread was his renown that Pope Leo XIII called him "the whole world's saint," and he has been a doctor of the Church since 1946. He was well known in life for his prayerfulness, learning, preaching, and pastoral care.

St. Jude, one of the Twelve surrounding Jesus, has an obscure biblical profile. That has probably helped him to become so cherished and his cult to be so flexibly shaped! His niche as patron of the hopeless probably has more to do with the twentieth century than the first. A Claretian priest found a prayer card in a church pew in the early 1920s, and he developed a personal devotion to the then-little-known saint. In 1929, as the Great Depression was starting, he and confreres began public devotions to St. Jude at their very poor church in Chicago. The Claretians soon began publishing *The Voice of St. Jude* (now *U.S. Catholic*) from Chicago. By 1937 thousands of letters were received daily, thanking St. Jude or making prayer requests. People who found St. Jude to be a powerful intercessor most often were women struggling (as their letters sometimes attested) with problems of husbands, children, health, finances, and the like. These devotees, so often facing hopeless situations, tried to combine their devotional outlooks with the stresses of a challenging world. Their devotion often brought them either constructive ways to take good steps forward or strength to endure troubles.[7]

29. What were the objections and approaches advanced by Martin Luther and the Protestant Reformation regarding devotion to the saints?

Martin Luther retained a certain respect for the saints all his life. Yet he made his opposition to then-prevalent ways of *honoring* saints a significant part of his reform. His views, more or less shared among the Reformers, proved crucial for the Protestant tradition.

Luther's ideas on saints and their cult were consistent with his main theological stances, as follows. He stressed that God is uniquely powerful and gracious. The saints should never be considered more like God than like their fellow Christians, sinful yet justified. No "works" (charitable deeds, penitential practices, devotional acts) of the saints or their devotees can bring about the right relation to God (righteousness) that comes to a person of faith as God's pure gift. Faith, according to Luther, is the saints' best possession and most imitable feature. To the extent that they lived by faith, saints inspire all to be receptive to Christ's work of making people righteous or just in relation to God (justification). Scripture contains the definitive Word of God and so serves as the norm for assessing the truth of doctrines and the value of practices. Many practices of honoring saints are not commanded or suggested in the Bible.

The Catholic ways of honoring saints, Luther found, served to distance people from God and to perpetuate an image of an angry God. Also, much devotion to saints seemed to him to take precedence over attending to demands of daily living. He was convinced that money going toward devotional practices could have been better used.

Following St. Paul, he broadened use of the word *saints* to mean also and primarily *communities* of living Christians. Since no one is deserving of the holiness that Christ gives Christians, it makes no sense to single out one or more persons to be specially honored, according to Luther's logic. The holiness of the saints, on earth and in heaven, is Christ's holiness applied to them and is nothing that they could earn or merit.

Luther held for remembering saints in moments of prayer to a limited degree. He allowed some prayerful gatherings to recall the saints on feast days, but he downplayed these. Saints he most admired were Mary, John the Baptist, Paul, Bernard, and Francis of Assisi, and these precisely for their closeness to Christ or for their pointing *away* from themselves *toward* Christ's salvation and graciousness. He wrote a moving commentary on Mary's Magnificat (Luke 1:46–55). There he focused not on her celebrated qualities or deeds but on her humility and especially her trust in a merciful God who acted powerfully through her.

Disgusted by false and overblown stories of saints' deeds and unlikely miracles, Luther nevertheless welcomed a kind of imitation of saints that emulated some saints who humbly admitted their need to be saved by God. Along with Mary, Francis of Assisi and Bernard of Clairvaux were clearly in this group. He found practices like honoring relics, participating in pilgrimages, and canonizing saints all to be detriments to adoration of God and to be fraught with self-seeking for salvation on the part of so many venerators. With what came to be characteristic Protestant respect for God's overarching majesty, he cautioned reserve regarding how much detail we on earth can know about the current existence of the saints in heaven.

30. What did Luther make of the practice of praying to the saints?

Luther's most important criticisms were aimed at invocation, which he ended up ruling out of Lutheran church practice. Martin Luther objected that, while the saints may indeed intercede for people on earth, there is not reason enough to invoke them on that basis. He saw invocation of saints as an abuse, since Christ alone is intercessor and savior. To call upon the saints, Luther claimed, is to engage in a practice lacking biblical support, and also to displace Christ by appealing to unnecessary go-betweens on the route of access to Christ.

In the 1530s, there were some attempts at a dialogue about the different outlooks, Lutheran and Catholic, on many church-dividing issues. But by the time of an official statement from Luther in 1538, his stance was set, with no turning back. While keeping open the possibility that saints in general pray for people on earth, he rejected invocation of saints. He (correctly) foretold that, without this way of honoring them, all the kinds of veneration of them would die down among his followers. One of his often-quoted observations says a lot: "When spiritual and physical benefit are no longer expected, the saints will cease to be molested in their graves and in heaven, for no one will long remember, esteem, or honor them out of love when there is no expectation of return."[8] Luther's stance provided the main thrust of centuries of Protestant opinion on prayer to the saints.

31. What was the Catholic response to the Reformation, and how did things play out in the centuries that followed?

As individuals and in organized colloquies, Catholic theologians responded to Protestant objections on the matter of the honoring, or "the cult of," the saints. Then, the Council of Trent (1545–63) taught about some aspects of the issue but did not attempt anything approaching a thorough treatment (to be provided only at Vatican II).

The theologians, as did the Council of Trent, generally reaffirmed established Catholic theology and practice of honoring the saints, although their statements show a concern that abuses in practice come to an end. Regarding invocation, the Catholic response at the time, from theologians and the Council, was continued endorsement, often with the concession that prayer can be made directly to God. Catholics saw invocation of saints as not taking away from Christ's unique role as redeemer and intercessor. It was emphasized that intercession and invocation happen only because of and with Christ, chief intercessor as well as our only redeemer and savior. Some prominent theologians advanced that while Christ is the only mediator of redemption, saints are mediators of intercession—but only with, in, and through Christ. They also proposed a few instances of biblical precedent for invocation. A main argument often put forward by Catholics was that since people on earth pray for one another and ask others for prayers, just as much or all the more should the saints of heaven be asked for their prayers. There was a sense of hierarchy conveyed; the saints were widely seen then to be closer to God than are people on earth.

In succeeding centuries, the Protestant tradition mostly distanced itself from the honoring of saints and especially from prayer to them, while for the Catholic side, the veneration and especially the invocation of saints remained a centerpiece of piety and a mark of a faithful Catholic.

The expression "cult of the saints," a legitimate one though sometimes interpreted pejoratively, has been used more by Protestants than by Catholics to mean the honoring of the saints. It has sometimes been confused with the word *cult* that means a kind of religious extremist group.

32. What was Vatican II's contribution to a strong understanding of the place of the saints in our lives?

The Council's core document on the Church, *Lumen Gentium,* produced the most systematic treatment of the role of heaven's saints in Christian life ever presented in official Church teaching. It is a concise treatment, found in four paragraphs of the seventh chapter of the document, but it offers solid theology and practical guidelines. Well grounded in the richness preceding it, this bridge chapter leads into the eighth and final one on Mary, mother of Christ and of the Church.

Lumen Gentium, like the Council itself, aims for unity and respect among Christian churches. Its ideas on the saints and their cult stay eminently faithful to Catholic teaching but also show awareness of the issues that had separated Catholics and Protestants for centuries.

Underlying the chapter's teachings are key ideas about the Church: a mystery, in the sense of a community in the world, made up of humans but filled with God's own life through the Spirit's presence. The Church is the people of God, those who live in communion with Christ and with one another. All the baptized, be they clergy, religious, or laity, are called to be holy and to take an active part in the Church's mission of word, worship, and pastoral care.

In paragraphs 48 to 51, chapter seven addresses the saints against the backdrop of the pilgrim nature of the Church as it moves toward future fulfillment. The holiness found already in the Church anticipates this final renewal. Among Christians on earth, all in heaven, and those being purified, there is a union, a solidarity, in Christ and in the Spirit. The saints in glory, close to Christ, stand as signs of the victory of God's grace. They contribute to the upbuilding of the whole Church through their holiness, their love, their example, and their prayer.

Christians on earth, the chapter teaches, can cherish the saints' memory and love them with a love that finds its end in Christ. Those on earth venerate the heavenly saints, look to them as models of holiness, and pray to them for benefits that come from God as their source.

The Council, toward the end of its treatment, cautioned about the possibility of abuses in the honoring of saints. Some abuses are of defect. Saints get too little attention, as when it is not grasped that the solidarity between the living and dead strengthens rather than weakens true worship of the Triune God. Other abuses are of excess, such as when efforts go toward too high a number or frequency of external practices rather than toward love of God and neighbor.

While groundbreaking, the treatment still left some unaddressed questions. The chapter does not provide consideration of the sense of distance from the saints and from the dead that is quite prevalent in much of the Western world. It probably can be interpreted as not mandating individuals' invocation of saints in their personal prayer, but it certainly gives a foundation for it.

The Council's thrust is away from a view of the saints as go-betweens and toward a sense of them as being in a true communion, a solidarity. This bond exists among all the dead who live in Christ, and the bond is centered in Christ.

33. Do the various Protestant churches now celebrate the saints in their official worship?

After centuries of widespread avoidance of, or opposition to, featuring saints in public worship, there has been significant movement of some prominent mainstream Protestant denominations toward greater celebration of cherished Christian figures. Notably this celebration is not limited to just the individuals or the categories honored by Catholics. Since canonization is not part of the practice of these churches, it is not surprising that the people remembered fit no clear set of criteria. The celebration of these deceased great ones tends far more toward remembering than toward invoking. Two examples are worth noting.

The *Lutheran Book of Worship* from 1978 serves some but not all of the Lutheran groups in North America. It provides for congregations using the book to commemorate, should they choose, particular people in various categories of notable deceased figures. Saints are among these, but they are a distinct group in a wide array of categories: martyrs, bishops, pastors, missionaries, renewers of Church and of society, theologians, artists, and scientists. The heroes included are from various Christian traditions. Invoking the saints for their intercession is not the aim here. The commemorations are meant to offer praise to God for impressive lives and contributions, to hold them up as examples of great faith and discipleship, and to inspire worshippers to live strong Christian lives too. There are other Lutherans who have not taken similar steps.

The Episcopal (Church of England) *Book of Common Prayer* from 1979 has feasts of Mary, angels and apostles, and also optional celebrations featuring many deceased members of the Anglican communion. It includes people of different gifts and circumstances, among them some Orthodox Christians and Catholics.

Evangelical Protestants typically do not mention the saints in public prayer or teaching, owing to concerns based in the traditional Protestant critique.

THREE

CANONIZATION OF SAINTS

.

34. What does it mean for someone who has died to be "beatified" or "canonized"?

When the pope canonizes a deceased Catholic, he definitively decrees that someone who is already beatified (declared "blessed"), in a separate but related multistep process, is inscribed in the canon (authorized list) of saints and is deserving of being venerated throughout the whole Church, in its liturgy and devotion.

Sometimes the process leading to canonization is called "making saints," a misleading phrase. The expression applies only in the sense that it is God who makes saints, with each saint's own cooperation, and with the help that Church members and others have shared with the saint. The Church, even though it spends lots of time and energy on procedures for investigating and judging a candidate's sanctity, does not so much "make" saints itself as it discovers some of those God has aided and welcomed into heaven. The Church sees the procedures involved as guided by the Holy Spirit.

A beatified person is one who, an official investigative process has shown, possesses a reputation for sanctity, and has either died a martyr for Christ or lived an exceptionally holy life. If that person is not a martyr, then as part of the process it must be determined that he or she has interceded with God in a way that has led to God's performing a proved miracle. The beatified person is considered a worthy model and an intercessor in heaven. He or she can be venerated limitedly, and (in the wake of post–Vatican II changes) can be a patron of churches and organizations. Beatification confers the title "blessed" on one who could be eligible to be canonized if one *more* (or for a martyr, in all *only* one) miracle attributed to his or her prayers is recognized.

Many bearing the title saint have never gone through extensive canonization procedures at all. That is because this category includes those saints prominent from the biblical period and the earliest Christian centuries. The process developed gradually at a later time, in the early and high Middle Ages; many saints were listed in the canon before there was much formality to being enrolled. Some others have undergone only part of the process. On the other hand, all those titled "blessed" did pass through it, for that title is itself a product of the official procedures that were not even in place for a long stretch of the Church's history.

It always must be emphasized that there are many more saints than those beatified and canonized. Being canonized and having the title does not make a saint any greater than another saint who is known surely to God but not to the world. However, it does make one's status as a saint official, and it places his or her life story before the whole Church, for remembrance, honor, imitation, and invocation.

35. What are the first steps along the way to canonization?

The road is long and demanding, and only a few candidates actually end up canonized. Before beatification, the procedure is likely to last years, decades, or even centuries. Frequently it takes just as long for a beatified person's advancement to canonized sainthood. Often the enterprise gets delayed or derailed completely.

The process, or more precisely the "cause," starts on the local level. A petitioner (a person or a group), impressed by a deceased person's outstanding holiness and hopeful for a determination that there has been a verifiable miracle involving that deceased one's intercession, asks the bishop of the would-be saint's diocese to open an investigation. That bishop has sole authority to introduce the cause or not, but he is expected first to seek advice from the bishops of the region, given the effect a beatification or canonization will have on the wider Church. If he agrees to begin, then with his approval the petitioner selects a "postulator" (one who would guide the cause through to its end). The postulator forms a list of witnesses who can be questioned for their honest remembrances and opinions, be they for and against the reputation of the deceased, traditionally called a "Servant of God" as the cause advances. The bishop also asks the Holy See in Rome if there are any known obstacles to the candidate's advancement. He also consults the people of the diocese about that. If all seems clear and he elects to continue, the bishop appoints a "promoter of justice." That person's role is to assure objectivity and make certain the process is fairly followed. That appointee also compiles a questionnaire for responses needed from numerous witnesses, as many as possible firsthand.

Then the postulator investigates for proof of heroic virtue or martyrdom and also assesses the candidate's reputations for holiness and for intercessory power with God. The postulator next carefully prepares and gives to the bishop a biography and a compilation of the candidate's published writings, if any. The bishop also appoints two theological consulters who consider matters of faith and morals relating to the candidate's life. After this comes a local investigation into the details of the miracle(s) attributed to the invocation of the candidate. This inquiry is made easier with the help of two experts, one theological and the other medical, under the leadership of the bishop of the diocese of the possible miracle(s). Near the end of this local phase, the bishop (or more probably his delegate) studies the evidence, and questions witnesses as needed. Finally the bishop decides whether or not to present the Acts of the Cause (the account of all the important information) to the Congregation for the Causes of Saints in Rome, which must accept the cause for consideration. All this comprises the diocesan inquiry stage.

36. How does Rome then get involved?

Next, Rome's Congregation for the Causes of Saints must study the Acts and appoint a "relator," located in Rome, to be an objective preparer of two *positios* (reports and summaries drawn from the Acts). One concerns the life and virtues or the martyrdom, and the other the miracles ascribed to the candidate. Then some cardinals and many officials of the Congregation study the *positios*. Finally, the pope reviews, consults, and either approves the beatification or not. The pope can intervene at any point, but he does not necessarily do so before this late moment. If all goes well, a ceremony of beatification then takes place, in Rome or elsewhere. This ceremony typically is not conducted by the pope, but Pope John Paul II preferred to preside in very many cases.

After beatification, so long as one miracle not previously considered is accepted and the reputation for holiness stays strong since beatification, then the cause can proceed to canonization. That calls for an even grander ceremony, at which the pope ordinarily presides. It traditionally happens at Rome, but recently it has been held sometimes in the saint's home country or region.

37. Why are miracles required, and what kinds of miracles are they?

Even if the candidate's life on earth was marked by the presence of miracles or extraordinary phenomena, that feature has nothing to do with the requirement of a miracle before beatification (except for martyrs, customarily) and another before canonization (for *all* candidates). This is because the miracles required are precisely those that happen *after* the death of a candidate, when praying people invoked the deceased one. The prayers and their corresponding miracles almost always concern physical healings, the easiest kind of miracles to examine. These miracles signify that the candidate is truly in heaven with God, interceding for God's granting of the miracle.

It has been customary for popes to hold that causes of martyrs need no miracle for beatification because, as we have seen, martyrdom has long been regarded as both a powerful show of God's power, and a sure indicator of the candidate's entrance into eternal life. Still, a martyr's canonization ordinarily depends on one proven miracle.

The last few centuries have seen the emergence of critical-historical methods and more sophisticated scientific investigations into miracles. This has allowed for much more precision than once was possible. Therefore, in advancing a cause, witnesses who can attest to the supposed miraculous response to a real need are important persons for the information they can offer the experts. If still alive, a person purportedly healed should be interviewed. The Roman investigators also view the reports submitted from the local scene. In addition, the Congregation for the Causes of Saints maintains a panel of medical specialists experienced with claimed miracles in causes. They subject the miracle claim to intense investigation and are especially mindful of ways in which seeming miracles may not truly be so. The Congregation thus benefits from scientific advances that save the causes from falling prey to unsophisticated explanations of healings. But it is not all science; the theologians also consider whether the miracle may be attributable to prayers to other than the candidate.

The number of miracles required has been reduced significantly over the centuries. A pope can dispense from the requirement of a miracle, but popes have not done that lightly.

38. How did canonization come about in the Church's history?

Canonization has a complicated history, with many changes in norms and procedures. The roots of the practice go back to when the early martyrs gave their lives for Christ, and lists were compiled locally with their names and dates of death. These official lists aided devotion and also served to disprove false claims about others who had not been martyrs. So, from the early centuries the Church guided the listing of these heroic figures, and various local churches kept records in the interest of proper and regular veneration. Cherishing and enshrining of relics (body parts) became an important part of venerating martyrs. When bodies of martyrs were moved ("translated") to a location of honor, a ceremony was held. Spontaneous popular acclaim accounted for martyrs' veneration, but by the fourth century the local bishops solely approved the public veneration and the addition of saints to the official lists. Local churches increasingly expanded their lists to include martyrs from other places, and this created greater need for vigilance concerning who should and should not be approved. Abuses were inevitable, and questionable figures had gotten mixed in with the rest.

After the age of the martyrs, as people began to venerate holy nonmartyrs, local bishops started to give approval to the cults of many of these beloved deceased. Those venerated figures who garnered reputations for performing or interceding for miracles while they were alive gained greater chance of being approved than did others. In the latter part of the first millennium bishops authorized cults of saints, but still in response to already strong devotion from the faithful. The authorization depended on no investigations or historical research. Still, criteria necessarily developed. These concerned a figure's reputation for notable sanctity, shown in piety, humility, and other virtues. These ordinarily also had to do with a reputation also for connections to miracles and extraordinary phenomena. Cults of the saints spread more and more beyond local confines, and so the number of honored saints grew. Bishops had to come up with some ways of restraining cults that were not well grounded and were prone to exaggeration or falsity. Until near the end of the first thousand years, the pope still did not get involved in the granting of approval.

39. When and how did the pope become more involved in the canonization process?

The first canonization solemnized in a papal ceremony was probably that of St. Ulrich in 993, declared a saint just twenty years after his death by Pope John XV. At that time, however, papal participation was neither necessary nor usual. During the next few centuries, as papal power advanced in the church, some but not all canonizations probably were led by popes. It is likely that popes blocked a few, too. The twelfth century brought the first instances not only of biographies prepared before canonization but also of commissions formed to inquire as to the fittingness of the proposed actions. In the thirteenth-century *Decretals* of Pope Gregory IX came the ruling that *only* a pope could canonize, and that he would do so only after experts conducted a full examination of witnesses. By the fifteenth century, beatification had been introduced as a step toward canonization, as a way of separating those deserving of local veneration from the canonized, worthy of worldwide honor. Increasingly formal and courtroomlike procedures came into place.

Separate regional listings of saints, with many saints common to most lists, gave way by the sixteenth century to the Roman Martyrology, a uniform Roman calendar for universal use. Pope Sixtus V established the Sacred Congregation of Rites in 1588, and part of its work became the oversight of beatifications and canonizations.

The sixteenth century's Pope Urban VIII collected all existing laws governing canonizations. This made it easier for Pope Benedict XIV, a century later, to issue a five-volume work that spelled out the Church's theology and practice of the process. Most of this material was still in place when the *Code of Canon Law,* containing hundreds of canons on the causes of saints, was promulgated in 1917. Without loss of a judicial framework to the process, Pope Pius XI set up an historical commission within the Congregation of Rites, and this group added a heightened note of historical methodology to the proceedings.

For centuries, it took the Holy See's action to get a process underway; a diocesan bishop was not in a position to do that. The twentieth century saw the initiation of the procedure moved to the local church and bishop.

40. You haven't said anything about the "devil's advocate" in the proceedings. Does this mean there no longer is one? If so, how else has the canonization process changed in recent times?

The well-remembered "devil's advocate" was one who, in the long canonization process marked by a highly judicial approach to investigating candidates, tried to muster arguments *against* the candidate's advancement. Thus, the devil's advocate (always a cleric) was envisioned—in obviously exaggerated imagery—as speaking up for the devil in the very process that was meant to point to those in heaven! With the change to a more historically based method of proceeding, following Vatican II (1962–65), this role ended.

The Second Vatican Council strongly affirmed honoring the saints but took a reforming approach to aspects of their veneration. So it was to be expected that the canonization process would receive some updating. Pope Paul VI issued his apostolic letter *Sanctitas Clarior* in 1969. This resulted in a new congregation with its own specific focus: the Congregation for the Causes of Saints. With that, a diocesan bishop could now introduce a cause (the less juridical and now-favored term, replacing process) but only after permission was received from Rome.

Pope John Paul II approved a new *Code of Canon Law* for the Catholic Church in 1983, and it reduced the number of canons on saint-making to just one. Fuller directives were provided in the apostolic constitution *Divinus Perfectus Magister,* also from 1983. It stipulated that the diocesan bishop can introduce a cause without explicit permission of the Holy See. Beatification and canonization became more closely linked in a continuum. The judicial tone of saint making, while not altogether dropped, yielded to an emphasis on historical inquiry. A former fifty-year wait after the death of a would-be candidate before introducing his or her cause has been lifted. This does not mean that quick proposals should be the norm, but it does allow greater flexibility.

In the centuries of the devil's advocate and the courtroom style of process, the candidate for sainthood was expected to conform to a pattern of sainthood that was more or less preestablished and reflective of the prevailing culture's sense of what is "heroic sanctity." For the most part, the standard measure of holiness throughout that long time was the set of virtues stressed in manuals of Scholastic theology: the theological virtues of faith, hope, and love, as well as the cardinal virtues of prudence, justice, temperance, and fortitude. Evidence of these virtues was sought in the candidate, and where the devil's advocate found these lacking, the candidate would incur criticism that begged refutation from those arguing for that one's advancement.

With the newer norms of recent decades, indications are that the more historical approach seems to at least slowly have made inroads. In this approach, Christian virtues are still sought. The life story of the saint has been able, more recently, to be composed and then evaluated in a less stylized way, one that does not demand that the saint conform so much to preset norms. The deeds, circumstances, gifts, and struggles of the candidates probably have a greater chance to be considered in themselves. Holiness to an heroic degree is still sought.

41. Why does the Church have these procedures at all?

This question can be answered on a few different levels. From the point of view of theological insight, causes for beatification and canonization function in the Church to give what is meant to be a clear and important message that the grace God offers his people is splendidly victorious. God's grace has in some particular people (not only the beatified or canonized but *all* saints) been exceptionally well received. Those "processed" are meant to be seen as just some of the ones who can inspire us; they point to the other, less acclaimed but true saints and even more to God's life, available to all. The canonization process reminds us also that life with God in the glory of heaven is real, and it underscores that God wants eternal happiness for everyone. The Catholic Church has long prized the principle that those called to a life of relationship with God in Christ and the Spirit can grow in holiness. Canonization emphasizes this truth and calls attention to its being an observable phenomenon, much more than just a tenet of faith.

From the perspective of the Church's mission of evangelization (spreading the good news of God's blessing and saving us), the Church's provision of models for holiness allows the real lives, actions, and heroism of the saints to speak loudly. Their witness is meant to assure and challenge us on earth to the heights of holiness.

From the viewpoint of the need for order in the Church, these connected processes help the Church to discern which figures are truly with God in glory. Given how important it is that examples of holiness be held high for all to see, the procedures keep the Church from honoring the wrong ones! History has shown that people can go toward shallow models and counterfeit signs of holiness.

All this is not to deny that these procedures are at least somewhat controversial.

42. Many people esteem the saints, but even some of these people are uneasy about canonizations. What makes canonizations controversial and unpopular among some people?

Various criticisms have been advanced concerning the wisdom and advisability of canonizing at all. Some Christians find saints to be irrelevant to their lives. Others consider them unnecessary given the central role in salvation of Jesus Christ. Also, we live in a world that often debunks any kind of hero, and this feeling can spill over to knock saints off their pedestals.

The cost of canonizations, in finances and also in labor, is certainly daunting. It has been argued that the money, time, and energy could more fittingly go to charitable or missionary endeavors. Like finances spent on Church art or architecture, funds used for canonization are meant to highlight the beauty and glory of God. In the case of saints, this happens through their shining witness. Not all would agree that spending so much money is worth even the attentiveness to the resulting beauty and saintly example that most would concede enhances the life of the Church.

Some object not to canonization itself but to aspects of its procedures, which are admittedly complicated. Being a human as well as a divine project, it is subject to bureaucratic tie-ups, biased judgments, politicking, and the like. The workings have a less-than-automatic quality to them, for the Church has to limit who is beatified and who is canonized, and it has to do that in view of its assessment of which messages about holiness most need to be expressed to the people of the present and future Church. The decisions, actions, and opinions of many different people are involved, and where eyewitness accounts are difficult to gather or judge, there is an obstacle to advancement. So, the process is bound to be inexact, even as the Church does not shy away from the claim that it is guided by the Spirit of God.

43. Why do some prospective saints get through the process, and not others?

First of all, it is important to stress again that the Church does not say that the canonized are the *only* ones in heaven with God. Canonization is not only a statement about the one canonized; it is also an act of the Church to proclaim a message for a specific age and through a particular life story. It is an aspect of the Church's telling its good news. The world's needs for saintly exemplars vary somewhat from age to age and area to area. It is only normal that there have been shifts in the profiles and kinds of saints considered valuable to canonize.

The advancement of a cause depends on human judgments of some key people, especially would be petitioners to the local bishop, the local bishop himself, his advisors, and the officials in Rome. Before accepting a cause for consideration, a local bishop considers how worthwhile it will be for the Church and the world if the long and demanding project would be undertaken and sustained. With consultation, he thinks about which saintly figures might be good to hold high in the Church and world of the present and the future. Who is to say which messages gleaned from which inspiring lives will best be worth investing so much time, energy, and money?

Religious orders especially, but also Church organizations and movements, often have been in a privileged position to promote a candidate, since they can draw on the resources of their members to support the cause for canonization of someone who may have been a leading member or even the founder. More than other supporters of a candidate for sainthood, some religious orders and Church groups have had the funds and the freedom to spend hours in long-term commitment, often over generations. They also have talent available to them, evidenced in knowledge of an order's history and charism, as well as in assignment of members with scholarly expertise. Money is held in common within religious orders; that money is sometimes at hand, not burdened by paying taxes or supporting dependents, and dedicated fully to the Church's mission. Finally, religious in consecrated life are people particularly called to witness to holiness, both in their individual lives and as part of communities. So, helping holiness to be noted and honored is part of their very call from God.

In reverse, particular categories of candidates for canonization have had harder times moving through the process. Notable among those who have not easily progressed to canonized status are popes, published theologians, and leaders of governments. Since writings and reputations need to be examined, these kinds of figures stand open to criticism being levied against their many teachings or positions.

44. Why do Catholics canonize only Catholics? Could other great people, such as Mahatma Gandhi or Dr. Martin Luther King, be so honored in the Catholic Church?

Canonization in the Catholic Church has always been only for Catholics, and it will probably remain that way. The Catholic Church is slow to make statements about people of other faiths, even about other Christians. Since points of doctrine and religious practice are investigated in the cause of the Servant of God, it would be difficult to come to a fair conclusion about a person not a Catholic, whose beliefs would be at least somewhat different from Catholic ones.

This issue has new import, however, after the achievement of Vatican Council II, which taught that authentic elements of the Church of Christ are indeed found in other Christian churches. That insight has made the connections between Catholics and other Christians intriguing and unmistakably worthy of respect. After all, a common belief in Jesus Christ as Lord and Savior is no small point of agreement in a world full of other beliefs, and of many people for whom religious beliefs make little impact.

If the day does come when some Christian figures that are not Catholic come in for some kind of recognition for their holy lives, perhaps then the recognizing body would represent a combination of Catholics and other Christians. Their discussions would probably be very interesting and filled with different perspectives.

Both examples cited in the question provide us with models of inspiring believers in God and, in the case of Dr. King, a Protestant minister of Christ. Concerning canonizing non-Christians such as Mahatma Gandhi, it would be odd for the Catholic church to presume to categorize people beyond Christianity in terms of Christian sainthood, which itself is defined in view of the life in Christ. Since canonization asserts that a deceased one is enjoying eternal life with God in the communion of saints, or Body of Christ, it would be odd for the Catholic Church to consider the sanctity of non-Christians, for whom the communion of saints is not a belief. That is *not* to say, however, that God's desire that all be saved and that all enjoy life with God forever does not extend to those deceased of other faiths. The important principle that the canonized are *not* the only saints of heaven must be remembered in considering many aspects of the honoring of saints. It certainly applies here, as we consider revered non-Catholic Christians and non-Christians.

45. Does the Orthodox tradition, devoted as it is to veneration of saints, have a process of canonization?

In each of many different self-governing Orthodox churches, a synod (or official group) of bishops has the ability to officially recognize particular holy people as saints; this rather simple process is not called canonization but rather "glorification." Since the Orthodox churches do not recognize the Catholic pope or have a corresponding overseeing figure, this method seems to fit their church structure.

This approach is a rather recent one, instituted in order to avoid abuses. The synod's recognition is emphasized as being a ratification of the people's own acclaim of figures as holy and in heaven. Sanctity in a human person is stressed as being the work of God's mercy and grace.

For the Orthodox, there is no elaborated and usually drawn-out weighing of evidence and examination of reasons. When the bishops gathered in synod declare the deceased to be a saint, three actions typically occur. First, a prayer service for that saint is commissioned to be written, an icon is arranged to be painted, and a feast day is established on the calendar. Second, a solemn ceremony, the "glorification," is set to be celebrated in a cathedral or throughout many churches. Then, on the designated evening, a requiem is observed for the saint, followed by an all-night vigil. Third, the next morning, the Divine Liturgy is celebrated, the saint's icon is unveiled and carried in procession, and a hymn of glorification is sounded. Although this set of happenings is common, a church need not go through it to acknowledge a saint; it would be enough to include the saint into the church's calendar. The fact of glorification by one church does not mean that the honoring of that saint necessarily should happen in other churches.

The Orthodox emphasize that the juridical bent of the Catholic Church's canonizing saints is missing from their procedures, rightly considered rather mystical in tone. This is because they highlight God's free action to sanctify or "divinize" the saint.

46. Do other religious groups canonize?

They do not. This is not too surprising for non-Christian religions for, after all, the word *saint* does not carry the same meaning it does in Catholicism. No other religious group, Christian or not, aims to single out deceased inspiring figures in nearly as detailed and universally binding a process as does the Catholic Church.

Among Christians, most Protestant churches would tend to shy away from such a process owing to their characteristic sense of belief that humans cannot know the mind of God. The Catholic willingness to trust in a process of assessing virtue and judging extraordinary phenomena (miracles) takes an approach to God that many Protestants would avoid. The classic Protestant emphasis is that God is far above us in knowledge and power. Canonization seems to allow too much of God's own wisdom to be fathomed by the Church. Some Protestant thinkers might also be reluctant to canonize on account of a profound sense that, after all, it is God's grace that saves us and not our own merit, and so the holiness of no Christian stands out or should be acclaimed as extraordinary when compared to the unsurpassed holiness of God. While in recent decades, committees or assigned members of some Protestant churches have presented well-researched lists and descriptions of heroic figures, these compilation projects do not have nearly the weight among their own members that the Catholic process is meant to have.

47. How many saints were beatified and canonized by Pope John Paul II, and how does he compare to previous popes on this score?

John Paul II's statistics are astounding. While he served as pope, from 1978 to 2005, he beatified 1338 deceased Catholics, 1032 of whom are martyrs, and personally presided over all the 147 ceremonies that marked these beatifications. He also gave the title saint to another 482 people. These were canonized in 51 ceremonies, all at which he presided. Of this number, 402 are martyrs.

There are fewer ceremonies than honorees because the numbers of those to be canonized or beatified were high. Combined ceremonies made sense, particularly when there were similarities among the honorees. In fact, many of the saints were beatified and canonized in groups because they were linked with one another in life and, in many cases, suffered death for the faith together. The huge martyred groups include 103 Korean martyrs (canonized in 1984), 117 martyrs of Vietnam (in 1988), and 120 martyrs of China (in 2000).

A comparative view shows that Pope Paul VI (1963–78) canonized 84, a number that held the record until John Paul II's papacy, and a number far higher than that of his predecessors over many centuries. Going back in time from Paul VI's papacy, we see that John XXIII (1958–63) "made" ten saints, Pius XII (1939–58) thirty-three, Pius XI (1922–39) thirty-four, and their predecessors from 1592 to 1922, a total of 236. To put it simply, John Paul II has beatified and canonized more people than all the popes of the past *four centuries* combined!

It ought not surprise us that John Paul II became such an exponent of honoring holiness in this way. As Archbishop of Krakow, he helped advance causes of many candidates for sainthood.

48. Why did John Paul II publicly recognize so many "blesseds" and saints?

Chiefly, he wanted to stress that holiness is for *everyone,* of every culture, country, and class, including people from the most ordinary of life's circumstances. He gives a further clue in his 2001 apostolic letter *Novo Millennio Ineunte* (On Entering the New Millennium), where he writes that holiness "has emerged more clearly as the dimension which expresses best the mystery of the Church. Holiness, a message that convinces without the need for words, is the living reflection of the face of Christ" (#7).

John Paul II was himself a bishop active in the Second Vatican Council. In its paramount Dogmatic Constitution on the Church *(Lumen Gentium),* the fifth of its eight chapters treats the "universal call to holiness"; that is, the truth that all the baptized are called to be holy and to participate in the active life of the Church. Many pastors and teachers have observed that this teaching, while often acknowledged as essential, needs to be more widely and better understood. No doubt John Paul II saw it that way too. In *Novo Millennio Ineunte* he looks back at that conciliar teaching and reminds the Church that "since Baptism is a true entry into the holiness of God through incorporation into Christ and the indwelling of his Spirit, it would be a contradiction to settle for a life of mediocrity, marked by a minimalist ethic and a shallow religiosity" (#31). He wanted also to make sure that contemporary people do not see sanctity as necessarily connected to some saints' extraordinary experiences, as if holiness were only for a few. He went on to say, "The time has come to repropose wholeheartedly to everyone this high standard of Christian living: the whole life of the Christian community and of Christian families must lead in this direction" (#31).

Underlying all this is the late pope's conviction that God gives people what they need to achieve holiness. If God is doing that, and if some people are wholeheartedly open to God's grace, then the Church should do its part to note publicly and officially many of the holy ones who are very likely to inspire Christians now and in the future. He held to a strong sense of both God's blessings and peoples' ability to respond to them in lives of holiness.

Procedurally speaking, John Paul II was able to beatify and canonize more people (and do so more efficiently and in a less costly way) because of the 1983 changes in canonization that he himself set in place. Historians and theologians replaced juridical officials (including the devil's advocate), while more attention was placed on the insights and efforts of the local bishops.

John Paul II's record-breaking "saint making" seems to parallel his unprecedented traveling to so many different countries. The two practices came together in that the pope often beatified and canonized people who lived in or near places he visited. Previously, Rome had been the only site for these, and until 1971 (with Paul VI's beatification of the martyr Maximilian Maria Kolbe), popes generally did not preside over beatifications. Both the honoring and the traveling reveal John Paul II's flair for the dramatic. He valued expressing the power of holiness at times when, and in places where, he thought the message might best be heard.

John Paul II's regular practice of personally presiding not only at canonizations but also at beatifications may have had the effect of leading some people to think that beatifications were indeed canonizations. Benedict XVI seems to be retrieving the custom of leading only canonizations. While he keeps his predecessor's tradition of holding the beatification ceremonies in diverse places worldwide, he looks to local bishops to lead these festivities. This change might help to highlight the difference between the two designations.

49. Have the great figures of the Old Testament been canonized and placed on the calendar of saints? Their names never seem to be prefixed by the word *saint*.

This is a pertinent question. More than in the past, recent awareness of the Bible has seen Catholics speaking of Old Testament figures as saints and naming children after them. The canonization process, developed long after biblical times, has not been used to examine any Old Testament saints, although there are many. This is because they had been placed on the Catholic Church's roll (canon) of recognized saints, the Roman Martyrology, before the process came about gradually at the end of the first millennium. Included in this number are figures like Abraham, Moses, Elijah, Isaiah, and David, as well as Adam and Eve, but also many more. Each has a date assigned, but the liturgical calendar for the universal church does not include any Old Testament saints, except those who may be listed on particular local calendars or on those of religious orders; for example, Elijah the prophet, who is beloved in the Carmelite order as a spiritual father.

Jacob Voragine, a noted thirteenth-century compiler of saints' lives, held that Old Testament figures should not be commemorated in the calendar. This is because they, having died before the coming of the Messiah, spent time in that place of waiting ("hell") into which Christ descended after the crucifixion to save those hoping for salvation. Whatever might be thought of his opinion, it was influential.

FOUR

MARTYRDOM

50. Some saints are martyrs. What qualifies them for this designation?

A martyr suffers death for devotion to a cause. *Christian* martyrs die for their allegiance to Christ's person and cause. At its root, however, the word *martyr* has a considerably less specific meaning: "witness," from the Greek *martys,* "one who testifies, as in court." Only occasionally in the New Testament era, but very much in succeeding centuries, a martyr meant one whose witness to Christ led to an endured death. That meaning gained hold as known Christians would be sought out and asked, "Do you believe in Jesus Christ?" That question, when met with refusal to compromise, sometimes led to a death sentence.

For Christians the term reflects, too, the evangelist Luke's use of it to denote one who has seen (witnessed) the risen Christ. When the word was applied to those who died for their faith, this later usage drew on Luke's sense and conveyed that martyrs had the power to give their lives because they had experienced the strength of Christ's resurrection.

In what became the Church's classic understanding of a martyr for Christ, three conditions are needed. First, there must be an actual death, and not just intense suffering or willingness to die. Second, the death must be inflicted out of hatred for faith in Christ and for allegiance to his life and his message, and not just hatred for ideas or works not explicitly Christian. Third, the death must be freely accepted. While this is the classic understanding, there has been considerable flexibility in defining and applying the term.

"Confessors" is the category for those who, under threat of martyrdom, confessed their allegiance to Christ but did not end up enduring death for that. They were given an honorable place in Christian memory. The term has come to designate nonmartyr saints in general, but it is not frequently used in this way.

Far more Christians went "underground" or fell away from the practice of faith than went bravely into martyrdom. Some others came close to being martyred but then could not stay faithful to Christ when the hard question came. Many Christians of their own era thought that those who reneged would be condemned to eternal punishment. Some today might tend to think that way, too. The truth, however, is that only God can definitively judge anyone, and God sees what no human being sees.

51. Was Jesus a martyr?

He certainly was. However, Jesus was not called one at the time of his death, and we don't ordinarily place him among Christian martyrs since he is the unique master for whom so many of his disciples have died.

Jesus, the ultimate witness to the Father, was consecrated by God and empowered by the Spirit. He gave testimony at his trial before Pilate (John 18:33–37) to the truth of his Father's kingdom. His witness to the point of death, life-giving for all, overcame the powers of evil. Jesus is "the firstborn of the dead" (Rev 1:5). Ministering amid misunderstanding and opposition, Jesus became more and more aware of the prospect of his violent persecution and death but also of the saving effect that his death would have for all God's people. Jesus did not seek out this fate, but he went willingly toward it. His attitude is notable and exemplary. Though innocent and sinless, he was treated like a criminal. When he could have become bitter, instead he showed love right through to his death. On the cross, he prayed for his persecutors: "Father, forgive them; for they do not know what they are doing" (Luke 23:34).

Christians see the resurrection as vindication of Christ's claims to be the Son of the Father and also of his message. Christ began to be called a martyr only in the second century AD at the start of the age of the martyrs. This was just after the term was applied to Saint Polycarp, bishop of Smyrna, whose death was seen as giving his life in a completely loving way that replicated in various details Jesus' approach to death.

52. Besides Jesus himself, are there biblical figures and themes that set the stage for the martyrs of the early Christian persecutions?

Yes. In the Old Testament, fearless prophets spoke and lived the message of God, who called them to their role. Their bearing witness to the truth of the Law came to convey willingness to die for it. Jeremiah 26:8–11 tells of the prophet being rejected with fierce words: "You shall die!...This man deserves the sentence of death because he has prophesied against this city." The prophet Uriah (Jer 26:20–23) was indeed killed for speaking God's word. Second Kings 9:7 shows that God sides with the prophets: "I may avenge...the blood of my servants the prophets, and the blood of all the servants of the Lord."

In 2 Maccabees 6:18–31, there is the moving story of the killing of heroic Eleazar, prepared to die willingly and nobly for God when confronted with an order from the king's officials to disobey God's laws. The next chapter (7:1–42) describes the witness of seven young brothers and their mother. Their freely embraced martyrdom inspired others to keep faith in God alive.

While martyrs' stories are not plentiful in the New Testament, there is a clear sense that witness involves not only loving, in deeds and not just words, but also holding to truth and resisting sin. Jesus himself was a witness to truth. As John teaches (15:16), the Holy Spirit, bearing witness concerning Christ, will speak through the mouths of Christians when they would face these challenges. Hebrews 12:4 implies that Christians will have to resist to "the point of shedding [their] blood" in their "struggle against sin " In Matthew 10:17–25 is the insight that Christians must expect suffering if they are going to follow Christ; there also is the assurance that God will provide support during such trials.

Stephen, the deacon, is known as the protomartyr, the first Christian martyr and one exemplary in mercy toward his persecutors. As recorded in Acts 6:8—7:60, he was tried before the Sanhedrin and suffered death for his allegiance to Christ; this occurred around AD 33.

The Book of Revelation also alludes to martyrdom (12:11). Its text, read at Mass on All Saints' Day, tells that those in heaven are there owing to the "blood of the Lamb [Christ]" and "the word of their [heavenly Christians'] testimony" unto death. At the Last Judgment, martyrs will become the judges, sending idolaters into deathly punishment (21:8).

53. Martyrdom is commonly thought to have happened continuously and everywhere in the first few centuries of Christianity. Is this an exaggeration, and how widespread really was martyrdom in this era?

We now know that this depiction is at least a bit exaggerated. While reliable statistics are not available, there has been of late a clearer sense that martyrdom was sporadic, and high in numbers only in particular instances and places. Still, the age of the martyrs lasted from the time soon after of the death of Jesus and the spread of the faith, until the fourth century, when Roman Emperor Constantine ended Christianity's illegal status and finally made it the established religion.

Contrary to some ideas recently held about Christians, they did not spend most of their time in the catacombs, and pagan tormentors were not constantly hunting them down. The Roman people certainly enjoyed spectacles in the amphitheater, and lots of victims were fed to the lions. Christians, however, actually made up only a fraction of those killed in this fashion. Although Christians usually were able to live in peace and safety, violent mobs were responsible for the death of Christian martyrs before AD 249. The terrible emperor Nero killed many Christians in

Rome, including probably Peter and Paul, about thirty years after the crucifixion of Christ.

When Pliny, the Roman governor, asked advice around AD 110 from the Emperor Trajan concerning how to deal with the emerging presence of Christians, the emperor told him to leave them alone unless particular Christians' behavior led to them specifically being denounced. That seems to be what happened to Saint Ignatius of Antioch, a prominent and outspoken bishop martyred at Rome. In mid-second century, Smyrna's eighty-six-year-old bishop Polycarp was killed there. Justin and companions were martyred in Rome around the same time, and many died in Gaul (today's France) at Lyons and Vienne. Scilla and Carthage were places that saw the shedding of Christian blood, as small groups there were martyred, among whom were Perpetua and Felicity at Carthage.

Martyrdom built on the situation in which Christians were a people set apart from the mainstream. They refused to worship the gods of the state. Half-truths made the rounds in Roman circles, rumors that in Christians' closed gatherings they were taking part in incest, cannibalism, and fornication. Even after much research, however, it is not clear on which grounds most of the martyred Christians were singled out to suffer their cruel fate. The theory that Christianity was an illegal religion, once roundly held, has been called into serious question. Were it true, it would leave us with the question of why just a comparative few were martyred. In times of outburst, however, Christians were indeed seen as public enemies. In this period, killings of Christians were "few and far between," although sad and notable when they happened. Precisely because martyrdom was drastic and not common, martyrs became heroes.

From AD 249, matters got worse in many periods and places. Laws were enacted to promote persecution of Christians. Emperors Decius, Valerian, Galerius, and Diocletian conducted organized campaigns. At times, Christians were commanded to turn over their Bibles for burning or to offer sacrifices to the pagan gods; their refusals sometimes led to death.

After the Peace of Constantine (AD 313), there were far fewer Christian martyrs, but there were outbreaks. Up to and including recent times, news of martyrdom has been heard, especially in missionary lands and in places where the Church's message is in any way a threat to established practices.

54. What is the meaning and value ascribed to martyrdom in the Church?

Mainly, it is that martyrdom imitates the death of Jesus the Savior, whose suffering and death give life. Martyrs witness to the belief that Jesus Christ is Son of God and is victorious over death and sin. Early Christian theologians offered various interpretations of martyrdom and principles for understanding it. Some became widely held.

From the epistle called the *Martyrdom of St. Polycarp* (ca. AD 156) comes the conviction that martyrdom is God's gift, not a purely human attainment, not something to be self-planned, and certainly not an escape from life's trials. The examples of Polycarp and Quintus are contrasted. Polycarp went into hiding from the emperor's officials, but he stayed with the people in his pastoral care and did not flee Smyrna. When found and questioned, he refused to deny Christ. His famous words flowed out: "For six and eighty years I have been serving Him, and He has done no wrong to me; how, then, dare I blaspheme my King who saved me!"[9] Quintus, on the other hand, turned himself in and tried to convince others to do so as well. However, in the end, Quintus lost his strength. He denied Christ and offered incense to the statue of the emperor.

The straightforward and paradigmatic *Martyrdom of St. Polycarp* conveys the idea that martyrs can bravely face their torture when it comes, because they are deeply in communion with Christ. Origen's later and influential *Exhortation to Martyrdom* (ca. AD 235) offers the ideas that martyrs love God so much that they fittingly become detached from the material and bodily world, that their devotion to God is so strong they appropriately drink from the same cup of suffering from which Jesus drank, and that their form of death can have saving value not only for themselves but for others. Still later, St. Augustine, in his "Letter to Festus" (AD 406), taught that "the cause [i.e., commitment to Christ, the reason behind the action], not the suffering [in itself], makes genuine martyrs."[10] This oriented people to focus on the virtues of the earthly lives of martyrs.

In the second and third centuries, many Christians held that the dead had to wait until the Last Judgment before they could be in God's presence in heaven. Martyrs, however, were held to be an exception to this, for they died as did Christ. Many accounts show that martyrs, while alive but close to the point of being killed, were likely to receive various signs of God's favor, such as visions, dreams, and ecstasies.

Frequently, the suffering of the martyrs was explicitly described as Christ suffering with them in their torture. In a celebrated martyrdom account, Felicity, a pregnant slave woman, shows the power of Christ at work in someone from society's fringe. As she awaits her fate and also gives birth prematurely, she proclaims eloquently that while she is suffering now, at her martyrdom Christ will be suffering in her.

Since the earliest centuries, martyrdom has been viewed as having an effect like that of baptism, itself a sharing in the death of Christ or a dying along with Christ. The nonbaptized martyr's death for Christ has long been termed a "baptism of blood," involving remission of sin and assurance of heavenly reward. For an already-baptized person, one who has sinned since receiving that sacrament, martyrdom has been seen as a kind of "second baptism" with its taking away sin.

55. How important have the martyrs traditionally been as inspirational figures in the Church?

Martyrs soon became the very archetypes of sainthood. Christians conceived that the first Church leaders, the Twelve, must have died as martyrs (other than John, the one notably reprieved from martyrdom); in fact, little is known for certain of how they died.

Theologians have seen martyrdom as a clear show of fortitude, a cardinal virtue and a gift of the Holy Spirit. It can show itself in two different ways: endurance and attack. The martyr is the exemplar of endurance.

The theological tradition holds that martyrs — because they are possessed not just of this courage but more basically of great faith, and also because they are motivated by a love for God that has grown strong throughout life — can be brave when presented with the choice between accepting death for Christ or not. Martyrs teach that life on earth is a cherished good, but that God is an even-higher good. Life here is short compared to eternal life with God.

To those in the Church, martyrdom is the Christian life perfectly ended. Martyrs show and prove the Gospel's truth and the higher power of God over creation.

56. What kinds of flexibility have stretched the application of the term *martyr*?

Christians killed under various conditions, and whose lives and deaths served to inspire others, often have been considered martyrs. The New Testament's Holy Innocents, infants slaughtered by King Herod in his search for the infant Jesus, have been celebrated as martyrs since the fifth century even though at the time of their deaths there was no "Christian faith" yet for them to believe in, nor had they reached the age of reason at which they could have chosen freely to die. In medieval Russia, a victim of political assassination was usually accorded the title of martyr; notable among these were the blood brothers Sts. Boris and Gleb from the eleventh century. St. Thomas à Becket, the twelfth-century archbishop and statesman killed at Canterbury in England, died for reasons that can be interpreted as religious or political or both. When medieval Christian sovereigns died warring against pagans, they frequently received honors accorded martyrs. Maria Goretti is "a martyr of chastity"; she died in 1902 in a botched attempted rape for refusing to give up her virginity. Maximilian Kolbe has been considered a "martyr of charity" for voluntarily placing himself in the stead of a soldier about to be killed at Auschwitz in World War II.

An interesting question arises: Do some surely committed Christians, suffering death in politically charged situations, actually die for their *faith;* or do they die for their *political views?* Indeed it is hard to say at times. Many now hold that the classic sense of Christian martyrdom needs to be expanded officially to include those who endure death for their prophetic stances based on their Christian beliefs, even if those positions embroil them in political disputes.

The twelfth-century Cistercian abbot-theologian St. Bernard of Clairvaux introduced distinctions still useful for stretching the concept. He singled out three kinds of martyred people: (1) martyrs in will and act, as in the three established criteria for "classic" martyrs; (2) martyrs in act only, such as the Holy Innocents, who could not choose their fate; and (3) martyrs in will alone, such as the persecuted St. John the Evangelist, traditionally counted among the martyrs, but not actually martyred.

Bernard's third type embraces the many confessors of the age of the martyrs. They suffered for loyalty to Christ but never were killed. Those imprisoned and destined for likely martyrdom were held in high esteem for their heroism and holiness even while they were still alive. Some Christians confessed their sins to these revered ones, with the sense that, once "martyred," so full of God's power were these holy ones and so able to intercede with God after their death for the sake of their repentant fellow Christians. that any sins told them would be forgiven. There was an assurance that God would never spurn their intercession. Confessors became the model for ascetics (people who exercise Christianity by spiritual lives of impressive discipline, as they "die" to selfishness and sin). The intriguing term *white martyrs* (as opposed to the red of shed blood) arose to describe inspiring figures who were not physically killed but who confronted their personal sin as witnesses to the power of Christ. Their heroism, in dying to the forces working against Christ while they kept on living for Christ, was seen as a continuation of the martyr's radical commitment in an age when physical death for Christ had mostly ended.

There is today a fuller sense of the unity of faith with social justice and peace. But this awareness rests on strong foundations. Saint Thomas Aquinas considers whether faith alone is the cause of martyrdom. In answering that the Beatitudes teach that "blessed are those who suffer persecution for the sake of justice" (Matt 5:10), Aquinas supports the Christian tradition that the martyr is one who dies for faith or another Christian virtue.[11]

57. Has the narrowness of the concept of martyrdom been challenged lately?

Yes. A good case in point is the brutal killing of late-twentieth-century Archbishop Oscar Romero in his own country of El Salvador in 1980. While celebrating Mass, he was assassinated for his courageous stand on issues of social justice. He did not have a chance to reaffirm or deny his faith just before dying, yet he witnessed his faith daily by continuing to celebrate Mass in his local church and by speaking out for justice. He was strongly resented. Hated not by "pagans" but by many from his own Catholic background, Romero was slaughtered not precisely for his allegiance to Christ but for his Christ-inspired opinions, most notably how the plight of the poor needed to be alleviated by allowing them a chance to own land they worked so hard to cultivate. The fittingness of terming him a Christian martyr would lie in his social-justice views that came largely from his understanding of Christ. On the other hand, some Christians, notably ones of his own country, would argue that his ideas and actions were primarily political, not religious.

The great fourth-century bishop St. Ambrose held that *truth,* no matter who speaks it and what it concerns, comes from the Holy Spirit. That insight has been invoked to argue for the status of martyrdom for deaths of figures like Archbishop Romero.

There is a martyrs' chapel in the Canterbury (Anglican) cathedral in England; it honors twelve who died as prophets and who might be considered martyrs in the stretched sense of the concept. Included are the Lutheran pastor Dietrich Bonhoeffer of World War II–era Germany, Martin Luther King of the United States, and Romero.

Recent decades have seen their full share of killings of Christians whose allegiance has brought them into conflict with opposing forces, usually in situations of extreme systemic injustice and oppression of the poor. More recent killings often are different from the classic martyrdoms. Death is often quick, such as by a hired assassin. As with Romero, steady witness in dangerous circumstances is usually part of the story, rather than one particular instance of interrogation. The moment for a single, considered, conscious choice may well not be there. This was the case for Sisters Maura Clarke, Ita Ford, and Dorothy Kazel, and laywoman Jean Donovan. They were four Americans willing to live for and serve Christ in the charged atmosphere of late-twentieth-century El Salvador. They met their deaths together on December 2, 1980, and from their story many people have come to think more deeply about how Christ's message touches social structures today. Some have called these people martyrs for Christ; perhaps they are, at least in an extended sense.

58. In the mainstream of Christian life, is there much awareness of martyrs now?

Despite the honor accorded martyrs throughout especially the earliest centuries, an awareness of martyrs has probably waned in recent decades, as suffering has been viewed less as a privileged path toward union with God than as a burden. The places and circumstances of martyrdom may be too far from the concerns of many people, especially those in more prosperous countries. Also, as greater attention has gone to the choices and interior dispositions within heroes and impressive people, the martyrs—many of whose thoughts we cannot know well unless they notably wrote or spoke before dying—present less content for reflection than do many other saints.

Pope John Paul II worked hard to hold martyrs high as exemplars. In his 1993 encyclical *The Splendor of Truth (Veritatis Splendor),* he presented the martyrs as models of moral living for their complete love for God and for living truthfully unto death. In the pope's travels, he chose to beatify or canonize many martyrs, whose life stories and heroic sufferings he hoped would inspire people both near and far from the martyrs' locales. After all, for those who understand it, the impact of martyrdom on the ongoing life of the Church is powerful. Testimony not with words alone but with willingness to suffer death can be forceful in prompting people to consider the values for which a martyr accepted death.

In fact, martyrs have a lot to teach us today. They show that the messenger can be killed, but the *message* cannot. They remind us all that ideals are needed in life. They also get us thinking that today's idols need to have worship withheld from them. The martyrs help us face a twofold question: What is worth living for and dying for? They show the importance of being messengers not just by words but by attitudes and especially deeds.

Christ's people comprise a "Church of the martyrs." The martyrs' experience, patterned on Christ's own death for our salvation, is that of believing so strongly that even death cannot squelch the intensity of faith, hope, and love. The mission Christ gave the Church is one of loving in a way so kenotic (self-emptying) that the world is transformed. Martyrs love to the extreme extent that they endure death for that to which they have committed their lives. They love others even when those others do not value the love being offered. They give themselves to the Lord and reach out to those the Lord would have them befriend, even when those they love insist on treating them as the enemy.

59. Have there been martyrs along denominational lines within Christianity, and have there been attempts to take an ecumenical view of martyrdom?

Amid tensions between divided Christian groups, martyrdom sadly happened, as in sixteenth-century deaths provoked by tensions and especially doctrinal divisions among those calling Christ their Lord.

In the ecumenical spirit that has grown over the past decades, Christian churches have tried hard to find ways of celebrating their own "confessional martyrs," ones martyred for a particular confession or church within Christianity. At the same time, however, these churches have looked for ways to respect the *commonality* that exists among them, to lament the interconfessional violence behind martyrs' stories, to hope for unity and growth in understanding, and to point all to Christ, the common savior of Christians. Christians remember the forgiveness that Jesus and Saint Stephen had for their persecutors as incentive for mutual forgiveness among churches. There have also been calls for mutual recognition of martyrs; this kind of proposal is a hopeful one yet also problematic, in that many martyrs have died for particular beliefs distinctive to their own churches.

Vatican II reminds us that the unity Christians share, centered in Christ, is greater than the differences between the churches. That being true, the witness of living justly will inspire across denominational lines.

FIVE

_____

HAGIOGRAPHY, OR THE LIFE STORIES OF THE SAINTS

60. How did saints' life stories begin, develop, and make their mark?

Hagiography (from the Greek, meaning "writings about the saints") has been greatly influential, and in the Middle Ages it proved to be the most prominent kind of religious literature. Much of what we know as history from the beginnings of Christianity to medieval times is known only thanks to hagiographical texts. The genre goes far back. Early Christians, devoted to the martyrs, composed martyrologies (lists) and also short "acts," "passions," and "martyrdoms." All these are related kinds of reports on the martyrs' trials, sentencings, and executions. These texts, along with letters and exhortations to martyrdom, retained their influence over the years and inspired Christian commitment. When the age of the martyrs ended, deceased holy monks and nuns who had practiced penance, fasting, prayer, and charity became, along with the martyrs, subjects of a new body of literature: *vitae* (Latin, meaning "lives," "life stories," or "biographies"). Two fourth-century works at the head of this genre are, from the East, *The Life of Antony* [of the desert] by St. Athanasius, and, from the West, the widely read *Life of Martin* [of Tours] by Sulpicius Severus; these became models for many other profiles of saints.

Soon, a pattern of common descriptive features came to mark most of these "lives," often with monotonous similarity. These included "signs of God's favor at birth, precocious holiness in childhood, renunciation of the world, struggle against the devil, fixed forms of asceticism, virtue, miracles, a death foreknown and joyfully embraced."[12] These common traits subtly expressed a valid point: that there is one holiness that flows from Christ and is a sharing in the life of Christ, whose own life for the most part set the pattern.

Monasteries functioned as centers for reflecting upon and handing on hagiography, since monks strove to be worthy heirs of the martyrs' and earlier ascetics' deep commitment to Christ through a kind of spiritual death—to the world and sin. In monasteries, legends were read for various overlapping reasons: as prayer, as moral guidance, as private devotional reading, as sources of religious education, as literary models, as mealtime edification, and indeed as entertainment. Martyrologies were lengthened from simple lists to include also information on the burial and on the place of origin of celebration. *Vitae* also provided the stuff of talks and hymns. Painted depictions of saints came to be considered a visual but true form of hagiography.

As the Middle Ages (476–1500) went on, saints' stories became widespread but subject to more and more embellishment. The legends reached lots of people, especially since many short accounts of martyrs and other saints were gathered together in "legendaries": multivolume collections arranged by saints' feast days, January to December. The East saw many more lives of the saints written than did the West, and Eastern collections were central to devotion; these collections were called synaxeries (short biographies) and menologies (longer bios, but not long enough to be a "life"). Although both freestanding and collected lives together dominated the body of literature on saints, hagiography embraced also lists of saints, personal prayers written to them, and liturgical texts, as well as inscriptions and accounts of relic transfers.

61. But didn't these stylized legends also end up distorting the truth about the saints and distancing ordinary people from them?

Indeed, the legends kept alive a particular sense of holiness that held strong for centuries, one filled with the saints' extraordinary phenomena. This presented a high ideal, easy to honor but hard to imitate—for it painted an unreal world. Miracle stories, which began early in the Middle Ages and flourished throughout that long era, did the same. These were filled with marvels caused by saints' interventions and often through the presence and power of their relics; they kept readers' attention and certainly fueled admiration of saints. These tales of miracles became the main content of many of the medieval lives of the saints. The word *legend* (from the Latin *legendum,* "what ought to be read") was used for a brief intriguing story, often about a saint; eventually it came to suggest a *far-fetched* story.

This increased emphasis on astounding miracles over the course of the Middle Ages shows in the contrast between St. Gregory the Great's *Dialogues,* a famous work of hagiography from the sixth century, and the Dominican Blessed Jacob Voragine's thirteenth-century *Golden Legend,* a day-by-day collection of much-abridged lives. Gregory's stories are, typical of his time, full of miracles, but they are interspersed with teaching about the power and goodness of God, the importance of charity and pastoral care, and the need for people to turn from bad deeds. The much-later *Golden Legend* uses the *Dialogues* as its main source, repeats very many of its miracles, but crucially leaves out almost all the moral and theological content.[13]

62. Since these legends presented such an unattainable ideal, it's only natural to ask: Why were these medieval lives written and passed down, and why did they focus so much on the miraculous? Did this trend eventually die out?

These stories were written to edify readers and to build faith, as well as to inspire Christians to praise the saints and ultimately follow them to heaven. These lives taught lessons more than they provided fodder for imitation of saints. Incorporating some historical truth, authors were deliberately selective. They presented saints as virtually perfect and suppressed discrediting information. In general, this resulted in plaster-of-paris saints, figures blandly portrayed as if wearing an impersonal mask, admirable people not very relevant or attractive. Sometimes legends were needed by locales that were repositories of relics of saints long dead to give a boost to the value of those possessions. Cleverly composed legends met that need even if details had to be invented or borrowed from other saints' stories! Any borrowing was not considered plagiarism, but a sign of reverence for the writer and also for sanctity's being "of one piece," not much different from saint to saint.

As need arose and grew for being cautious about which deceased Christians joined the Church's list of saints through canonization, the purpose for writing saints' lives expanded to include proving holiness. Understandably, lack of concern for getting facts straight only increased in this environment. As criteria for being canonized became tougher, lives of saints became more miracle-centered and stylized. Stories of saints often got conflated as authors tried to present saints to fit the Church's sense of what officially made a candidate qualify. The character flaws and personal struggles got pruned. Writers apparently hoped that lives would be more acceptable to authorities if not so tangled with temptation, effort, and conflict.

A less extreme hagiography did eventually arise. The roots of a more scientific, objective approach lay in calls that were sounded by some Catholics and more Protestants in the Reformation era. They urged getting the facts right and avoiding exaggeration. Reforming voices, like the Catholic Desiderius Erasmus (1466–1536) and the Protestant Martin Luther (1483–1546), asserted that many existing lives of the saints were limited and contained information hard for the reasonable mind to accept. Luther held that too many of these stories emphasized the wrong features about the saints. Where he wanted to find accounts of saints' faith, their humility, and their admitted need for God's help, he was discouraged by tales mixing stories of God's miracles in their lives with too many incredible stories of saints' outlandish traits and deeds. These, for Luther, worked to make saints into substitutes for God.

63. How did hagiography change after the Reformation?

Following Luther, the Protestant tradition looked mainly to the Bible to supply the narrative content of Christian teaching. Catholics, on the other hand, tended to keep prizing saints' stories, even when not all the details seemed quite trustworthy. Through the centuries since the Reformation, an increasingly well-educated Catholic populace cherished the saints and their stories, while some fine efforts were undertaken to separate "fact from fancy." The Enlightenment period brought skepticism about the supernatural but also an optimism about the capacity of scientifically conducted historical research to uncover truth.

In this vein, members of an always-small group of Jesuit priests—soon to be called the Bollandists, after their leader Father Jean Bolland (d. 1665)—began devoting themselves to accurate and painstaking research into saints' lives. Inspired by the idea's originator, Father Heribert Rosweyde (d. 1629), Bolland as well as his colleagues and successors have aimed to support the honoring of saints and to provide a scholarly collection of lives that would meet exacting standards. These Jesuit hagiographers faced opposition from those unhappy with some of the conclusions, especially religious-order members who disputed the researchers' reasonable assertions about their founders. Undaunted, the Bollandists steadily published volumes of the *Acta Sanctorum,* collections of well-researched lives first issued in 1643 and organized according to saints' days in the Church calendar; scores of volumes have since been published. In 1882, the Bollandists began issuing the journal *Analecta Bollandiana* to cover matters of hagiographical research.

Nineteenth-century advances in historical methodology, archeology, philology, and paleography allowed hagiography more sophistication. Still, there was considerable antagonism, now mostly ended, between scientific historians and pious defenders of the historical truth of legends. The former ridiculed much of the outlandish content of lives, while the former stuck firmly to what most people now would conclude is quite incredible.

Thanks to Alban Butler's eighteenth-century *Lives of the Saints,* many English-speaking readers have been exposed to scholarship about the saints in accessible form. The four-volume work, organized according to saints' days in the Roman Martyrology, was updated and improved in 1928 and again in 1956. Another recent and extensive collection of saints' lives is the *Bibliotheca Sanctorum,* begun in 1960 and finished in 1970. Written in Italian, it is arranged alphabetically by saints' names.

The Bollandist Hippolyte Delehaye (d. 1941), a master of critical hagiography, opened its insights to a fairly wide public, with whom he shared his sense of the most common errors made in trying to understand saints' lives. These included not separating the saint from the legend, trusting too much in the hagiographers, and being naive about details concocted to connect a saint to a place that badly wanted a link to one.[14]

The Second Vatican Council, with a nod to all these good efforts, briefly referred to hagiography. Concerning the Liturgy of the Hours, it is said that "the accounts of martyrdom or the lives of the saints are to accord with the facts of history."[15]

64. In the recent past, how influential on Catholics has been the reading of the life stories of the saints?

Until at least the mid-twentieth century, many adults and youth were exposed to the life stories of saints through various popular sources: books about particular saints, chapters or brief entries in collections, occasional sermons, and even a few motion pictures and comic books. In Catholic schools and in religious education classes for young people, stories of the saints often spiced up classes that otherwise were taken up with large amounts of memorization through oral drill of rather dry catechism answers. Those who prayed the Liturgy of the Hours (mostly clergy, seminarians, and members of religious orders) got used to short readings, many quite preposterous in content, assigned to the "second nocturn" (an "hour" prayed during the night) on a saint's day.

In the last few decades, there has been something of a downturn in the prominence of the saints in much religious education, partially owing to an upturn in attention to Christ, the Bible, and contemporary issues. Indeed, heroes of all kinds have become more suspect throughout contemporary culture. In a simpler time, the saints' stories were sometimes "the best game in town," holding their own with Westerns, fairy tales, war stories, and the like—all before the coming of the Internet, movie rentals, multichannel television, and media saturation.

65. Among scholars, what is hagiography's current status and importance?

Since the late-twentieth century, scholarly interest in saints' lives has been strong. This parallels new concern for those kinds of local and social history told "from the bottom up" that can supply data on ordinary life otherwise hard to find. This research, often conducted without a Christian faith perspective, continues to produce serious studies that typically focus on "the cult" of one or a few saints in a particular place at a particular time. These become important fodder for broader studies. More than in the scholarly world of the 1800s, the content of the centuries-old sources is respected, not necessarily for its religious truth as for revealing what people then thought, believed, and valued. The saints profiled in the writings often are studied less for themselves than for what society was like in the times when their cults flourished, or why in a particular era people were attracted to a certain saint.

Textual criticism offers insights but also tough challenges to understanding the actual saints. Many researchers hold that hagiographical texts do not offer reliable views into the saints, their society, or the spirituality of their era, because there are so many factors that influenced the texts' being written and so many layers of development. Some scholars lament that the saints, and people's reasons for loving them, may be nearly impossible to know. This situation is related to the status of historiography in general.

Recent historians, more modest than those of a few centuries ago, emphasize that history is prone to interpretation and that it cannot claim to be exact.

66. What are the characteristics of good hagiography for our times?

Hagiographers today may be either research scholars bringing their skills to analyze existing saints' lives, or authors producing new works of various lengths and levels of sophistication. These works may treat either long-recognized or recently identified saints.

Those hagiographers who study works from ages past should be expected to collect all pertinent material; to use methods uncovering background, purpose, content, and style of the writing; and to make sound judgments about evidence gathered. If this is done, then a fair assessment can be made of what is timeless and life-giving about a text, or not. In all this, it does no one much good to gloss over problems or, on the other hand, to focus narrowly on what is deficient in the person or story of a saint.

In writing new lives of saints long-recognized or recently canonized, wise authors strive for various ideals that need expression in their texts: a sense of God's having created, saved, and invited a saint toward closeness with God, love for others, and respect for self; a good grasp of the human condition, and especially of the dynamics of conversion from selfishness to growth in Christ; a sense of the reality of sufferings and struggles encountered along the Christian journey; and a feel for the needs and questions of the expected readership. Writing a saint's life is a challenging task. Historical truth must be sought and presented fairly, even if some readers might not like to read that truth. At the same time, there has to be attention to content that is distinctly spiritual, concerning holiness, values, and the like.

In short, lives of the saints fit for the present and the future will be those grounded in an enlightened psychology, expressed in an attractive literary style, filled with hope and joy rather than mainly discouragement and sadness, and focused on the true humanity of a person embraced and changed by the love of God.

67. *The Da Vinci Code* certainly places St. Mary Magdalen in an interesting light. Who really was Mary Magdalen?

Dan Brown's fictional *The Da Vinci Code* presents, with considerable originality, Mary Magdalen as the figure to Jesus' right in Leonardo Da Vinci's famous painting *The Last Supper.*[16] Art history and religious tradition see that person differently: as the young St. John the Evangelist. Furthermore, Brown writes of Mary Magdalen's being Jesus' wife, mother of their offspring, and the one intended to be leader of the young Church. Brown's interesting and best-selling story builds on a premise that is just not true. It must be said, however, that the evolution of the tradition about Mary Magdalen has begged a clarification and quite likely a correction—just not Brown's fictionalized one!

The Mary Magdalen of Scripture is the woman healed of demonic possession (Luke 8:1–3) and also the first witness to the resurrection (John 20:1–18). She later was admiringly called by Hippolytus of Rome, and then by St. Augustine, "the apostle to the apostles." That indeed is what Christians should find most significant about her, regardless of what else is considered to be in her story.

The basic problem in the Christian tradition is that the identities of several other women have probably been conflated with that of Mary Magdalen. Her being healed of possession, through early and repeated readings of this event, perhaps led to the interpretation that she was a sinner needing forgiveness, rather than a victim needing healing. This skewed her persona at least a bit and maybe a lot. So her profile has taken on facets of a few different women: the anonymous penitent sinner who anointed Jesus' feet with her perfumed oil (Luke 7:36–50), the woman caught in adultery (John 8:1–11), and, on a more sympathetic note, Mary of Bethany (Luke 10:38–42). Many scholars would now say that there is no convincing scriptural evidence to link her with any or all of these others.

The probable conflation began early on in biblical commentaries, stories, homilies, and works of art. Pope St. Gregory the Great, the sixth-century hagiographer, likely built on these interpretations and so saw Mary Magdalen as the reformed prostitute. In his pastoral concern and without access to resources now had, he no doubt saw a real advantage in stressing the transformation in Mary Magdalen, in her move to dedicated disciple. He was able to make an example of her to teach a lesson about conversion from sin to grace.

In the past decades, biblical scholarship has rehabilitated Mary Magdalen's image. Brown's popular book rightly points to the existence of misunderstandings through the centuries. He presents them, in his fictional work, as part of a campaign to smear her, and that makes for interesting reading. When taken as factual, however, his interpretation creates newer and bigger misunderstandings.

SIX

THE SAINTS IN LITURGY

68. Do the saints have much of a place in the official, public prayer of the Church?

Yes, they very much do, although their place is secondary to and dependent on God's. *Liturgy* is the name of the Church's official prayer, which uses texts and rituals set by Church authorities. Liturgy includes the Eucharist and all the sacraments, the Liturgy of the Hours, the liturgical year, and celebrations such as the funeral rite and the ritual for the dedication of a church. Liturgical prayer is offered to God both on earth and in heaven by the whole Church, the Body of Christ. The prayer takes place through Jesus Christ, Son of God, who intercedes (prays for) the Church to his Father. It happens also through the power of the Holy Spirit, who inspires and supports all Christian prayer. Since the saints in glory are part of the Church, they do what the Church does when its members pray to God. As Church members on earth join together for prayer or ask one another to pray for particular needs, so the saints in glory pray to God with and for the rest of the Church.

In the Church's liturgical life the saints are strong participants. They receive remembrance, veneration, imitation, and invocation. When we gather to pray in the Church's many different rituals, often we recall and honor the saints for all they have been and have done, but not apart from our greater remembering and honoring of God. In liturgy, we are moved to imitate them in daily life, since their qualities and deeds frequently are mentioned in prayers, readings, homilies, and hymns. Invoking the saints, we ask them to pray with us and for us to God, and we do this with a sense that they are in solidarity with us as we pray.

69. Do many liturgical prayers get addressed to the saints?

Most liturgical prayers are addressed to God the Father, with a few others addressed to the Son, the Spirit, or the Trinity. When

prayers are directed to God on a saint's feast at Mass or in the
Liturgy of the Hours, the saint is often remembered in any of a
few important ways: with joy that this holy one now shares life
with God in glory, with praise and thanks to God for the virtues
or deeds found in the life of that saint while on earth, in hope that
the lives of those praying may show these same virtues and deeds,
and in supplication that the prayers of that saint be offered to God
on behalf of those praying and those for whom they pray.

The Litany of the Saints is an unusual liturgical prayer since
it calls upon the saints directly. Found in liturgy as well as in popular devotions, it consists mainly in a listing of names followed
by a very brief and uniform prayer request (typically "pray for
us"). Even this direct beseeching of them, however, is framed
within prayer to God. The litany starts with the expression of a
few names or titles for God, each followed by the same brief
request for God's action. In its conclusion, the litany reverts to
addressing God and again asking God for aid.

The Litany of the Saints is used at baptism, since new
Christians are entering into a group of people who form a Church
wider than a community of any one place and time. Furthermore,
baptism celebrates God's calling his followers to holiness in
Christ, a holiness lived by the saints, who are models for us.
When baptisms or receptions into full communion with the
Church happen at the Easter Vigil, the Litany of the Saints occurs
then, and it should be sung, to convey the joy of the occasion.

The same litany finds its place in ordinations of bishops,
priests, and deacons; in those rites the candidates for ordination
prostrate themselves during the litany. In this way, someone about
to be ordained remembers his inclusion among all Christ's disciples throughout the ages. He is reminded also of both the central
role of holiness in ordained life and the exchange of spiritual
goods that can happen among members of the communion of
saints.

Other occasions calling for the Litany of the Saints are the consecration of virgins and the dedication of churches. A form of this litany is optional within the liturgical prayers for those who are dying.

70. In the Church's understanding of what the Mass is all about, how do the saints fit in?

The Mass can be described simply as memorial, sacrifice, and banquet. The saints relate to all three.

Memorial. At Mass we remember God's blessings, and our salvation from sin and death through the paschal mystery: Christ's death and resurrection. Different from other memorials, the Mass does not just remember Christ's presence but brings it about. Through Christ, we enjoy communion with God and also with all those who live in the Body of Christ, all sharing in his life as parts of the human body share in the whole. Though invisible to us as we pray at Mass, our worldwide neighbors worship and remember God with us, as do those awaiting the fullness of glory, and those already in glory, the saints. In the Mass, we remember the saints, who have communion with us now. We recall how they believed, struggled, and loved while they were on earth. We are conscious of all this within that larger memorial of Christ's paschal mystery.

Sacrifice. Christ's death on Calvary was a gift of himself to his Father and to us. It was the ultimate gift, for Christ accepted death on the cross for our salvation and to advance the kingdom of God. Christ's self-sacrifice makes possible the sacrificing love of all those alive in him. The martyrs sacrificed themselves for Christ because of their faith in him. All saints now in glory with God have joined the gift of their lives to Christ's own self-gift. We are called to do the same.

Banquet. In the Church, which is Christ's body of followers, members share in the richness that his paschal mystery has achieved: life eternal and the good things of the kingdom of God.

On the night before he died, Jesus hosted a meal and instructed his disciples to do as he had done: take and bless bread and wine, that these elements might become his own body and blood, through the Spirit's power. In continuity with what Christ did, the Mass is also a meal at which God spiritually nourishes us, Christ's invited guests. The Mass changes us and unites us more closely to God and to one another in God. When Christ comes again to complete the kingdom he revealed at his first coming, the banquet of heaven will be lavish and filled with Christ's friends. Already participating in the joys of heaven are the saints, friends of God, who have died and have been given the gift of glorious life. They, like us, await an even fuller banquet. The Mass—in its prayer, its message, its communion—provides us a glimpse here and now of the joy of our future union with God. In the Eucharist, the whole Church celebrates; those on earth join with all in heaven (saints and angels) to praise God. Saints thus give us hope as we pray with them at Mass.

71. Where in the Mass are the saints explicitly mentioned and remembered?

The Penitential Rite, when the Confiteor "option" is chosen, asks the saints to intercede for us as we acknowledge our sins and ask for God's mercy. *God* grants the mercy, but the whole Church—including the saints—prays for it. Wherever the Apostles' Creed is used for the profession of faith on Sundays and on solemnities (i.e., in some countries and at Masses for children worldwide), there is a list of beliefs that includes the communion of saints.

In any of many possible prefaces to the Eucharistic Prayer, the Father is praised and thanked for his work of salvation. Prefaces for days that honor one or a few saints make general mention of them. There are four prefaces for Mary, one each for John the Baptist and Joseph, one for Peter and Paul together, two for apostles, and one each for martyrs, pastors, and virgins/religious. There are two for the many saints ("holy men and women") who have no specifically designated preface, and one for the solemnity of All Saints' Day, November 1. At the end of many other prefaces (e.g., those for the Epiphany, Lent, and the Chrism Mass), there is either explicit or implicit mention of the saints. At the heart of the Mass, each of the many possible Eucharistic Prayers makes some reference to the saints in glory and rejoices in the communion shared with them.

In the Concluding Rite of the Mass, the presider blesses the assembly in preparation for sending its members forth to love and serve God. At this point, there is the option of using a longer Solemn Blessing, with twenty possibilities given in the Sacramentary, the official prayer book for Mass. Four of these, intended particularly for use in celebrations of the saints, are for the Blessed Virgin Mary, Peter and Paul, the apostles, and all saints.

72. Where are the saints included in the Eucharistic Prayers of the Mass?

Of the four major Eucharistic Prayers, the First (the Roman canon) contains the most elaborate and specific references. Before the consecration of the gifts, we "honor Mary..., Joseph, the apostles and martyrs." It then immediately names "Peter, Paul, Andrew," and—if the presider chooses—twenty-one other designated holy men: the rest of the Twelve, the earliest popes after Peter, and a few early martyr-saints. Toward the end of this same prayer come intercessions for the dead and the living, and then there is mention of other specific early martyrs. Those at Mass are asking God to bring them more deeply into union with him and into solidarity with all those who live united with the risen Christ. Here there is again a chance to make the list longer by mentioning eleven specific men and women, all martyrs from the Church's earliest centuries. Whether the list is longer or shorter, the phrase "and all the saints" completes it. Its use makes it clear that the saints abound. The "fellowship" sought is with all the saints.

The Second Eucharistic Prayer has its own preface, concluding with "And so we join the angels and saints in proclaiming your glory as we say…." It requests that our merciful God will "make us worthy to share eternal life with Mary, the Virgin Mother of God, with the apostles and with all the saints who have done your will throughout the ages." It leads us to praise God "in union with them" (the saints).

The Third Eucharistic Prayer immediately proclaims that God, "holy indeed," has in every age called people everywhere to be united in giving God glory. The implication is that the holy God calls all to holiness. Then, after the Consecration, saints are mentioned within the context of the Eucharist's being our way of joining Christ in making a self-offering to God. We pray: "May he [Christ] make us an everlasting gift to you, and enable us to share in the inheritance of your saints, with Mary…, the apostles, the martyrs," and either the saint of the day or the patron saint of the gathered assembly.

The Fourth Eucharistic Prayer rehearses the story of salvation history in some detail. Near the end it asks the merciful Father to bring us to heaven, "in the company of the Virgin Mary, the Mother of God, and your apostles and saints."

The Eucharistic Prayers for Masses of Reconciliation and Masses with Children generally include many of the same sentiments in similar or simplified language.

73. How best can the celebration of a saint's day be worked into the homily?

The General Instruction of the Roman Missal (abbrev. *GIRM;* last updated in 2002) offers a helpful explanation of the homily at any Mass: "It should be an exposition of some aspect of the readings from Sacred Scripture or of another text from the Ordinary or of the Proper of the Mass of the day and should take into account both the mystery being celebrated and the particular needs of the listeners" (*GIRM,* #41). Unfortunately, it can happen that not a homily but just a "talk" on a saint makes its way into the liturgy with little or no connection to any part of the Mass or the readings for the day. Applying the directions of the *GIRM* in practical ways offers a more appropriate, and actually a more holistic, way of handling it.

Usually the purpose of the homily is to "break open" the message contained in the readings in order to apply Scripture to the here and now. The readings themselves are contained within the wider celebration of the whole Mass, which has both its unchanging prayers and its "proper" prayers special to the day or the season. The homily must also pay attention to the fuller event being celebrated in feast and season. On a saint's day, it is not only fitting but desirable that the homily allude somehow to that saint, perhaps with reference to specific proper prayers of the Mass. If a tie-in can be made between the readings and the saint's story, so much the better.

For some saints' days, the Church presents designated readings that fit the life story and the message of the saint. The homilist is thus assisted by the readings in highlighting the day's saint. If a saint's particulars are not easy to link with the texts of the day, it might be better for a preacher to speak about the category of saint (e.g., martyr, apostle, doctor, religious).

Reference to saints in homilies need not be confined to their feast days. So long as liturgical prayer texts and biblical passages are respected, the life of a saint can be blended well into homilies at any time. Drawing too heavily on the saints as resources could result in imbalance or overload, but saints' lives and teachings are appropriate for preaching on any day.

74. In homilies, how can stories of the saints fit in with the biblical passages of the readings for the day?

Since the homily is meant to link biblical happenings thousands of years ago with the realities of life in our world today, the stories of the saints can be helpful for a homily—including one that is well-rooted biblically. This is because saints are examples of people who met timeless challenges. Their world may be as different from the biblical era as from ours, but still their stories show us how Scripture can be applied to any life story at any time to reveal the life-giving message of God. The story of the Bible is meant to intersect with the story of our lives. Bringing in a third story (that of a saint) can prompt reflection on both of the others (biblical and our own), and help us to make connections with the saints' own lives as well.

Sometimes there are legends about saints that seem rather far-fetched, to say the least. When a homilist, researching available information about a saint, finds stories that seem wholly untrue or in part factually questionable, that does not mean the legend is absolutely to be avoided. But "honesty is the best policy": admit what's far-fetched. Otherwise, intelligent listeners may think that the homilist or most worshippers base their faith on hard-to-believe tall tales. A legend may convey a message that is worth hearing, but only if listeners are not distracted by wondering if everyone else present (including the homilist) accepts the historical accuracy of the tale! These legends might have their place in homilies, particularly since they show something of the people who in earlier times had devotion to that saint and brought to expression, albeit exaggerated expression, a sense of God's power acting in that saint's life. A good rule of use might be to use such stories limitedly, with proper explanation, and with a quest for how they reinforce the authentic facts, valuable example, and ongoing witness of the saint.

75. How then would a homilist go about preparing a homily for a saint's day in a way that blends well with the rest of the Mass?

Professor of homiletics Father James Wallace advances a workable method for incorporating saints into liturgical preaching.[17] He presents three phases of preparation, all "to link the biblical story with our own story through the use of the saint's story."[18]

• *First phase*. The homilist considers the day's readings and prayer texts. This means reflecting on them personally, and then consulting biblical commentaries to discover what the scriptural passage meant for the people in its own time. The homilist moves on to think about what the same passage means for people now. For example, how does it confront or console them?

• *Second phase*. The homilist becomes mindful of "the mystery of Christ working in this specific [saint's] life."[19] Wallace proposes considerations for the homilist: "What lasting values of our tradition are found in both [biblical] text and saint? How does the saint's vision of living the mystery of Christ relate to the thrust of the text? What did the saint stand up for or against? How does the prophetic call of the text find embodiment in the example and accomplishments of the saint?"[20] Texts from Scripture and liturgy may be related to the saint's life or to just one incident, attribute, or quotation from the saint. The saint's life should enhance the Word of God.[21] One way of doing this is to view the saint as "a reflection of God." As Wallace says (p. 32), the saint's story "mirrors the face of God" (with "face" representing qualities like gentleness, passion, forgiveness, constancy). In doing this, the homilist alerts people to look at what God has done in this person. By showing the story of the saint and God's action within that story, the homilist aims to demonstrate God's love. Another way of using the saint's life to enhance the Word of God is to view the saint as an exemplar. The homilist here would focus specifically on the response made by the saint to God's invitation to be Christian in concrete circumstances. Obviously, a homilist uses both approaches and, in the course of many homilies delivered, varies the two.

• *Third phase*. The last phase of Wallace's plan calls for the homilist to reflect on the hearers' needs. Considering those, the homilist ponders: Is this day's saint someone whose story lets the Word of God come to good expression? Specific categories of people may benefit from hearing of saints like themselves. He notes that Elizabeth of Hungary and Margaret of Scotland were wives and mothers; Maria Goretti, a teenager; Elizabeth Seton,

a young widow; Monica, an older widow; Thomas More, a husband and father; Thomas Aquinas, Augustine, and Teresa of Avila,
seekers after knowledge and insight into spiritual growth.[22]

If hearers find themselves admiring only the saint's holiness and not seeing some personal connection, they may find it
hard to make a response. In fact, the very struggles against personal sin that saints have endured can make saints' stories helpful to people.

76. How do the saints' days fit into the Church's liturgical calendar?

The calendar starts on the First Sunday of Advent (late
November or early December), and it ends a year later on the
Saturday *before* the new First Sunday of Advent. The year is com-
prised of liturgical seasons; namely, and in this order, Advent,
Christmas, Ordinary Time, Lent, Easter, Pentecost, and Ordinary
Time (again). The Church year is thus cyclical; it follows this pattern annually and renews itself at each new Advent. The year is
structured around celebrations of the life of Christ. Advent has us
waiting to celebrate Christ's birth, while the end of the Church
year places before us the future event of Christ's coming in glory
as King. In between come important days like Christmas,
Epiphany, the Lord's Baptism, and Easter. We move from expectation of Christ's coming, to his birth, and then to his ministering,
his trial and death, his rising, his sending of the Spirit, and his living and acting in his Church through the Spirit's power.

All the events just noted are fittingly part of a temporal
cycle— from the Latin *tempus,* meaning "time"—for they move
from a start to a finish. Since this "timeline" traces the life of the
Lord Jesus Christ, and since the word *lord* in Latin is *dominus,* this
cycle is also known as "dominical." But the temporal/dominical
cycle is not fixed by the dates of the secular calendar, and here's
why: The heart of the liturgical year is Easter. The secular-calendar
date of Easter changes every year as it is calculated partially

according to lunar phases (because of its close relationship to Passover). Since the resurrection is the heart of the liturgical year, once Easter's date is set, the dates of all other liturgical events radiate out from there. Thus our understanding of the liturgical year gets more complicated (or richer), and the inclusion of saints' days adds another layer to that.

On each date within the secular year, the Church remembers many saints. Only a few hundred of these few saints either *must be* or *may be* remembered with specified prayers for liturgies on their assigned days. The liturgical commemoration of these saints comprises the "sanctoral cycle." (*Sanctus* in Latin means "holy" or "saint.") This cycle of dated saints' celebrations blends with and respects the seasons and days of the more primary temporal/dominical cycle; some dates in the sanctoral cycle actually celebrate the Lord (e.g., Christmas, December 25).

So, the liturgical year is made up of two fully overlapping and interwoven cycles, one temporal/dominical and the other sanctoral. These have existed since the early centuries. Throughout history the sanctoral calendar was adapted, at times reduced, and more often expanded.

77. Some saints' days of observance changed after Vatican II. How are days allotted to saints?

The arrangement of saints' days has been developing in the Church since its first few centuries. While every canonized, or officially listed, saint has a day in his or her honor, fewer than two hundred saints' days are actually observed in the general or universal *liturgical* calendar. This means that only these saints have liturgical observances, with prayers particular to them, that either *must* be observed (in the case of solemnities, feasts, or obligatory memorials) or *may* be observed (in the case of "optional" memorials).

Whenever a person has reached the point of being officially recognized as a saint, a date is assigned in the Roman Martyrology.

Given how many people are officially listed, every day of the year has many saints whose day it is.

Many possible factors affect the determination of a saint's date. The classic and often optimal situation is that a saint's day of celebration is the day he or she died. The day of death is seen as that person's day of birth, or entrance, into eternal life. For various reasons, however, this has not always prevailed. Perhaps the strongest reason is that the date of death is already taken up with another liturgical day of greater importance. Also, in some cases, the date of death is not known; saints from the earliest centuries naturally are less likely to have a known death date. Finally, saints from the last few centuries may have dates of death that were "already taken."

The post-Vatican II calendar-reform tried hard to bring dates of as many liturgically commemorated saints' celebrations as possible into line with dates of significance for particular saints when their dates of death were unavailable. Some other types of dates include the following: the date of burial (a close second behind the death date); a date near the actual date of death; the date of birth; the date the saint's body was transferred to an important location, usually the final place of rest; the date of dedication of a church in honor of the saint; a date celebrated in another rite of the Catholic church; or a date found on an ancient calendar.

In addition, following Vatican II's concern for the important focus on the paschal mystery of Christ in liturgical observance, some saints' dates were moved out of Lent to clear that meaningful, Christ-focused season of too many saints' memorials. Prayers on saints' days were made to reflect to some extent the seasons in which they fall; this is particularly the case in Advent, Lent and Easter.

78. Do saints' days of the liturgical calendar have different levels?

Yes, individual saints' days have various levels, or ranks. The current ranking replaces a similar but short-lived division of festivals into first, second, or third class; that one in return replaced a longer-standing, more complex system. So, post–Vatican II renewal simplified what had begun some years earlier. Currently the highest rank is a solemnity, a solemn or profoundly important observance. In descending order of importance after that come feasts, obligatory memorials, and optional memorials. Solemnities, feasts, and obligatory memorials must be observed in liturgy; most solemnities and feasts in fact celebrate not saints but rather God or a theme in salvation history. Optional memorials may be observed or not, and the choice ordinarily rests with the presider. Memorials, be they obligatory or optional, all honor saints, including Mary (and one is for the guardian angels).

Solemnities of the saints are rare; their feasts less so. Three solemnities honor Mary: in her immaculate conception (December 8); her being Mother of God (January 1); and her assumption (August 15). Two other solemnities fete particular saints very closely related to the Lord: Joseph (March 19) and John the Baptist (June 24, his birth; not his beheading). These three saints all have at least one other day that is not a solemnity in the calendar. One last solemnity, that of All Saints, honors those (perhaps very many) saints who are truly in heaven but lack official individual recognition as such.

Saints with feasts in their honor are Mary (her birth and her visit to Elizabeth); Paul (his conversion); the apostles Peter and Paul (their martyrdoms traditionally celebrated together); Peter (more precisely, the chair that symbolizes his authority); each of the Twelve (most by themselves, some coupled with another); each of the evangelists; and Lawrence (probably owing to his being a patron of Rome with Peter and Paul). Then too there are the martyrs' feasts on the two days right after Christmas: Stephen (the first martyr) and the Holy Innocents (martyrs collectively).

Three archangels—Gabriel, Michael, and Raphael—also rate a commonly shared feast.

On the universal liturgical calendar, memorials are, by far, the most numerous kind of saints' days; some are obligatory and many more are optional. Approximately sixty-five saints' memorials are obligatory worldwide, counting only once Mary (with many days under her various titles) and grouped saints (e.g., Sts...and..., St...and companions). Similarly counting, approximately ninety-five saints' days are optional memorials throughout the world, with special prayers provided in the Sacramentary, the prayer book for Mass, and in the Liturgy of the Hours. In a few of these cases, two unrelated saints share an optional day, something that does not happen with obligatory memorials universally celebrated. In these cases, neither saint *must* be commemorated, but only one *can* be.

79. How did Vatican II respond to the numerous celebrations of saints' days?

Just after the sixteenth-century Council of Trent, Pope Saint Pius V issued a general (worldwide) calendar that contained only sixty-five dates for saints' celebrations. By 1960, well over 200 of 366 dates had been given to required remembrance and honoring of saints in Mass, leaving less than half the days of the year for praying the important seasonal prayers of the Christ-centered temporal cycle. By the beginning of the twentieth century, with the overload of saints' days, the prayers for Masses on days as significant as the Sundays of Ordinary Time and the weekdays of Lent were rarely used. Several popes made incomplete efforts at calendar reform to lessen the number of saints' days.

Vatican II set things in place for a revision and reduction. Its liturgy decree, *Sacrosanctum Concilium,* gave the impetus: "...the Proper of Time [the temporal or dominical cycle] shall be given the preference which is its due over the feasts of the saints, so that the entire cycle of the mysteries of salvation can be suitably recalled."[23] On the importance of Sunday, the same document declared, "Other celebrations, unless they be truly of overriding importance, must not have precedence over this day [Sunday], which is the foundation and nucleus of the whole liturgical year."[24] Thus, it set things in place for feasts and memorials occurring on Sunday to yield to the Sunday celebration. A few paragraphs later come these words: "Lest the feasts of the saints, however, take precedence over the feasts which commemorate the very mysteries of salvation, many of them should be left to be celebrated by a particular church or nation or religious community; only those should be extended to the universal Church which commemorate saints who are truly of universal significance."[25]

To implement these and many other conciliar principles, Pope Paul VI set up the Concilium for the Implementation of the Constitution on the Sacred Liturgy *(Sacrosanctum Concilium),* a group that worked to produce *General Norms for the Liturgical Year and the Roman Calendar,* promulgated in 1969. The published norms referred to the need for the revision: "Of its very nature the liturgical calendar is changeable, and occasionally new celebrations have to be added, but admittedly over the past few centuries, the number of feasts has become excessive."[26]

With a sense of the centrality of Christ's place in the Church and in liturgy, along with a theologically substantial sense of the saints' function within the Body of Christ, the project moved in two directions: to cut back the overall number of saints' commemorations, but also to diversify the overall group of saints whose memorials would be included in the calendar—so as to let the full splendor of the saints shine more clearly. Indeed the project was not intended to diminish the importance of the saints in liturgy or in Christian life.

To bring about a reformed list of saints of the universal calendar, four criteria were used: (1) historical authenticity, (2) geographical diversity, (3) chronological diversity, and (4) universal significance.

80. After Vatican II, how did the historical authenticity of some beloved saints get called into question?

The Council called for respecting the results of historical research into saints' lives. Serious doubt about historical authenticity would keep a saint off the Church's universal liturgical calendar. Questions such as "Can we know with certainty that this saint actually lived?" and "Are we sure that what is claimed about this saint's life is really accurate?" became crucial.

In the case of certain saints previously in the calendar, it was conceded that the historical information about their lives was sketchy at best. In some cases, the conclusion was reached that a saint's historical life could not be recovered. Historical authenticity proved to be a seriously respected criterion for the revision. Many saints did not make the cut.

Some removed saints captured some significant media attention at the time. St. Christopher was dropped off the liturgical calendar because it became quite clear to experts that, although Christopher's cult (devotion offered to him) is long-standing, we know next to nothing about him. A famous and moving legend about Christopher (the name meaning literally "Christ-bearer") does not rightly deserve to be joined with the martyr Christopher. The martyr Christopher is presumed to have existed (given the cult), but the legend should not be linked with that martyr. With the legend stripped from his real story, his significance is much diminished.

Toward Philomena, another saint dropped from the universal liturgical calendar, great devotion had arisen, in part owing to nineteenth-century St. John Vianney's devotion to her. In decades before the revision process, excavators had concluded that the inscription in the Roman catacombs that had long ago been understood to bear the name Philomena—as a burial marker—is actually an admonition using words mistakenly taken to mean a woman's name. The martyr Philomena thus has been shown not to have existed, at least not as a woman martyred and then buried in that spot. Because of this, Philomena was dropped from the liturgical calendar. (Happily for anyone bearing that name, there are other saints named Philomena!) Unlike Christopher, she is out of the much longer list that is the Roman Martyrology, as she is no longer considered to have existed.

81. What was the operating principle underlying the application of criteria concerning geographical and chronological diversity?

The revision process had to take seriously a central insight of the Second Vatican Council, one taught in the fifth chapter of the Dogmatic Constitution on the Church *(Lumen Gentium):* that *all* the baptized are called to holiness, by a call that gets expressed in many different places, eras, vocations, and personalities.

Given how many biblical and early Christian figures have traditionally been numbered among those who must be liturgically included, it would be both difficult and inappropriate to upset the balance greatly away from early Christianity and the area of the Holy Land and adjacent Asia and northern Africa. Likewise, so many others are from Italy, France, and the rest of Europe, where the Church has flourished for so long. Despite this, as time moves along, of course, more saints join the number of disciples, and Christian life expands to areas before not as populated with Christ's disciples. So it made sense that saints be placed in the general calendar to represent the various places, periods, and ways of life that are meant to be fields in which holiness can be found.

In the end, the revision broadened the memorialized saints to more regions, but to a limited extent. Consider, for example, Charles Lwanga and companions from Uganda, Paul Miki and companions from Japan, Andrew Kim and companions from Korea, martyrs all. Groundbreaking as this move was, this is an aspect of the calendar that is liable to undergo increasing widening, whenever another revision might occur. For example, the

Americas barely came into the universal liturgical calendar. Australia and environs are not included at all.

From era to era within Christian history, different groups of saints have been prominent, and this is somewhat reflected in the calendar revision. A simple overview yields this summary: From biblical times come the figures who encountered the Lord. From the next few centuries are the martyrs and early monks. At the end of that period come bishop-theologians, hermit-monks, and the earliest monks in community. Into the Middle Ages there are wonder-workers and abbots of monasteries, and also a few missionaries and royalty, along with theologians and bishops. The late medieval period adds many founders of religious orders. The Reformation and Modern eras see many of these same groups, with an accent on missionaries, charity-doers, and founders of orders engaged in active ministry.

82. After the revision, how are the saints in the liturgical calendar now balanced out between men and women, and among various states of life, parts of the world, periods in history, and social classes?

Among the eighty-one saints of obligatory memorials (ones whose celebration days must be observed), there are fifty-nine men, not counting companions of Paul Miki, Andrew Kim, and Charles Lwanga. Counting Mary, Mother of God, just once, there are twenty-two women. In terms of percentage, that is 73 percent men and 27 percent women.

Geographically, approximately two-thirds of this group of saints come from Europe, with a high number of twenty-two from Italy. The rest come from Africa (specifically northern Africa, except for Charles Lwanga) and Asia (in and near the Holy Land, except for Paul Miki and Andrew Kim in the Far East).

Concerning clerical or lay status, ordained men who are popes, bishops, or religious-order members predominate. Women are almost all religious. Very few laypeople or diocesan priests are included. Just a few deacons make the list.

Centuries vary with respect to number of saints represented, but broad epochs all are there. Not surprisingly, the nod for highest numbers goes to the biblical period and the first few Christian centuries. The sixteenth century, a tumultuous time when reforming saints came forward for the good of the Church, stands as an example of a heavily represented century. Only approximately 14 percent of the saints derive from the seventeenth century or later.

If a search for upper, middle, or lower classes were made, it might be difficult to decide how to include those many in religious vows, or how to place a division among characteristics of class members. Making a rough attempt to look at the families from which saints of the universal calendar have come, it can be said that the upper class outnumbers the middle class, and the middle overwhelms the lower.

As these statistics could be used to argue, there will be need for revision of the calendar of saints from time to time. Who knows when the next revision might take place? Now that the Second Vatican Council's stress on the universal call to holiness has had decades to make inroads among theologians, pastors, and teachers, many eyes will be upon those charged with the revision.

83. Considering the concern for geographical diversity and universal importance, are there now differences for determining which saints get celebrated throughout the whole world?

The general calendar is to be followed worldwide, but provision is made for local calendars as well. These are not only for dioceses and religious orders but also for groupings of dioceses in provinces, regions, countries, or larger areas. Each local calendar respects the worldwide celebrations, of course, but it also adds some of its own festivals.

Some of the many saints' days that had been dropped from the general calendar were assigned to the local or particular calendars.

In many cases, days that are optional memorials throughout the world become obligatory memorials in the local churches where these saints carry a significance (usually as patrons of the country or former residents).

The revised calendar calls for a saint's day to be celebrated as a solemnity in a specific church or parish if that saint is the patron. So, if a parish is named for St. Catherine of Genoa, for example, her date of September 15—not even included on the liturgical calendar—would be a solemnity in that church alone. A whole diocese celebrates the patron of its cathedral and/or diocese as a solemnity too.

On a day when no other celebration must be observed, a group gathered for Mass can keep the memory of a saint. Doing so would be especially fitting on that saint's day or if the group has a special connection to the saint. This is true of saints both in and beyond the liturgical calendar. In the Sacramentary of the Mass, there are generic prayers to be used for the commemoration of a saint. Into these prayers can be inserted the name or names of that saint. Sometimes, too, prayers designated for a particular category of saints can be used, inserting the particular name of the saint who fits into that category. For example, St. Julia, a virgin and martyr of the early Church, can be remembered in liturgy, and her name can be inserted into either a set of prayers used for martyrs or one used for virgins.

84. How was the criterion of universal significance applied to the revised liturgical calendar?

This phrase from Vatican II's liturgical decree proved troublesome as the job of revising the calendar got underway, for it is challenging to resolve the question of exactly who is or is not significant to the *whole* Church! The category eventually was scaled back to a more modest phrase, "greater importance." Even then, agreement was hard to come by. To be sure, every list of important saints is going to be affected by the worldview and the outlook on

Christian holiness prevailing among the revising group. Is significance determined by the life and acclaim the saint received during or soon after his or her lifetime? Perhaps, but more probably and rightly it has to do with what the ongoing message of that life might say to people now. So, "significance" may shift as evangelizing themes change. New problems arise that call for inspiring witness of saints who show creative ways of living discipleship in holiness.

The group appointed by Pope Paul VI to revise the liturgical calendar presumably did their best to come up with a list. The pope, of course, must have had final say over the listing of saints to be included, and over the assignments of those to designations of obligatory or optional memorial. A pope can add or delete saints from the list of those to be remembered liturgically. He can move them from obligatory to optional or vice versa, but that is not done lightly. This is not only because it causes a lot of worldwide communication to spread the word but because the liturgy is not easily to be altered.

85. In all, how successful was the attempt to revise the liturgical calendar after Vatican II?

In a general sense, the saints became less prominent. Their days decreased in number. In other ways, however, saints' days were revitalized so that the days gained an added significance.

The effort to streamline numbers but broaden the types of the saints in the calendar was at least partly successful. The number of saints' days was indeed greatly reduced, while saints from different times and places were added. The celebrations of historically unverifiable or insignificant saints were dropped or reduced in rank (e.g., from obligatory to optional memorial). Dates of celebration were made to correspond better to liturgical seasons or to events of meaning in the saints' lives. Sundays were able to make their impact through proper prayers fitting to their seasonal placements.

The resulting lineup of saints, however, has come in for a good deal of criticism, first of all by scholars, who nonetheless acknowledge improvements have been made, and also by people in the pew. Average Mass-goers sometimes wonder why there are not more married saints and a wider selection from different parts of the world. Many commentators have held that the revision did not go far enough on various fronts. As the Church moves into the future, other revisions likely will happen, and that prospect gives hope that excellent models of holiness and universally significant prayer companions will be retained or added for the good of people throughout the Church.

SEVEN

THE SAINTS IN ART

86. It seems that so many pieces of art have saints in them. What explains their prominence?

Throughout Christian history, artists' renderings of saints in notable places within churches allowed people to honor those holy ones to whom they looked for inspiration, friendship, and prayers. Because the saints assumed such an important status in devotion, and given the illiteracy of so many people for so long, artistic presentations of the saints offered a popular, useful way for people to learn about their faith and its heroes.

Stained-glass windows, stone wall-carvings, statues, and paintings have graced churches for centuries. These pieces of art, even if not all excellent, functioned as "books," especially before the invention of the printing press around 1440. In many a great cathedral, or perhaps in a parish church or a monastery, one can still walk along and follow a series of related windows or carvings that tell a story or teach a lesson in some depth, yet without words.

Individual believers and families have prized pieces of art displayed in their homes, worn on their persons, or kept near them. These pieces can engage their minds and hearts in knowing the saints, their stories, and their teachings. It doesn't matter whether the work is fine art or not. More crucial is that the observing believer senses a link with the life, virtues, and ongoing love of the saint.

The practice of gazing upon the saints in art led to a way of quiet meditative prayer for the sake of imitating their portrayed actions or attitudes. Followers of the Devotio Moderna approach to spirituality (a late-medieval movement centered in the Low Countries) engaged in this method in respectful imitation of saints, and through it they sought their own moral growth. With a somewhat different goal, monks (e.g., Benedictines, Cistercians, and Carthusians) and mendicants (e.g., Franciscans and

Dominicans) more likely prayed in this way to achieve tranquility, focus in prayer, and a sense of greater communion with the saints viewed. Visual images engage people's aspirations and dreams, such that their ideals stay strong or get stretched a bit.

Visual imagery has played a huge role in Christian life, especially in the Catholic and Orthodox Churches. Despite the greater attention historians tend to give to written texts, religious art is not only enjoyable to view; it has a lot to teach, as many art historians and students of religion would attest.

87. As we look at art depicting saints, some objects appear to be symbols. How do we understand what the artists are trying to convey about the saints?

We probably cannot fully grasp artists' intentions, but that makes art intriguing! There are clues, however. Over the centuries, and in an elaborate way by the Renaissance era, fascinating patterns of depicting the saints came to be standardized. Major features of saints' stories or reputations became translated into fairly predictable symbols. Some generic symbols were matched with types of saints, such as palm branches with martyrs. Particular saints, especially the most popular ones, came to have their own more-or-less unique symbols. Even uneducated viewers could grasp the meanings of most symbols and so could glean what artists communicated about a saint's qualities, notoriety, and lessons to be taught.

Some symbols are objects of religious significance that the saint could well have owned, worn, held, or kept near. Other renderings are less realistic; they are not what the saint would have been seen actually having or holding while on earth. Still other symbolic messages are conveyed by artistic devices like color variations, size of figures, or placement of the saint within the scene.

Some individual saints are easy to identify, because of the presence of particular and clear symbols unique to each of them. More usually, symbols are shared by groups of saints or by a few different ones. Some detective work, such as noting which symbols are combined, can often reveal exactly who one of these saints is. More on the specific meanings of symbols is in the next answer.

88. What is the meaning of the saints' halos and other prominent symbols?

The halo (or nimbus) is usually a golden circle around the head. That circle stands for eternity—with no beginning and no end—and for the heavenly bliss the saint enjoys with God. The bright golden color represents the shining holiness of a saint. For Christ, the halo is often topped with a cross (sometimes called a "cruciform" halo). The beatified may be shown with a less demonstrative halo of shafts of light coming from behind the head. Early Christian freestanding statues were often provided with metal discs, usually gold-colored and shiny, attached to the heads.

Ancient pagan artists had shown important people by encircling them in light, and so the Christians took and adapted that custom. Closely related to the halo is the *mandorla* (Italian for "almond"), an almond-shaped light that surrounds the whole body and may be framed with points of flames or doves. This attends mostly Christ, the Trinity, and Mary, although it has been used for showing saints ascending into heaven.

From other artistic symbols we can glean more about the saints than might first meet the eye. The basics of this symbolic "language" can be learned, although there are enough technical details, variations, and ambiguities to keep the study of saints in art an involving pursuit.

Some symbols are common and their meanings reliable and clear-cut. For example, models of church buildings usually designate bishops or founders who served there. A lamp, a candle, or a lantern all stand for wisdom and piety. Armor or swords are often used for soldier-saints. An anchor epitomizes patience and hope, and a skull both penitence and awareness of death. A chalice indicates faith; with a serpent in the cup it is a symbol of wisdom. A branch of the lily points to the chaste life of either men or women saints. Dragons or monsters represent heresies or controversies with which the saints battled. Long robes are common for desert monks, as are habits for members of religious orders. A book or scroll often indicates evangelists, doctors and teachers, popes and bishops.

Other symbols are trickier to decipher. For instance, a sword is a sign of a warrior-saint, but as a banner, it might mean death by violence. A soldier-saint might also be given a flag with a cross unfurled, but so might a missionary. Flames of fire may indicate martyrdom, but they may also imply loving dedication. The lion indicates the practice of holy solitude when it is found near desert monks, but also courage in the face of persecution when it accompanies martyrs.

89. Can you give a brief history of the saints in art?

The saints have been featured in art since the rise of veneration of the martyrs and of their relics. Reliquaries (containers for relics) were often adorned with pictures of the saints whose remains they held. As devotion to the saints increased from early Christian centuries through the Middle Ages, the saints' inclusion in Christian art kept pace. That should not surprise us, for people have a natural inclination toward artistic expression, and religious folks have long taken to depicting God and their heroes. Early Christians filled catacomb walls with drawings of scenes from the Old and New Testaments and with symbolism that still intrigues both scholars and tourists.

After the fourth-century establishment of the Church as the official religion of the land, more and more church buildings were erected. With that, pictures and statues of saints became quite numerous. Stained glass, mosaics, frescoes, statues, liturgical objects, and carvings all were possibilities for featuring saints in portraits or scenes.

Especially in the East but also in the West, there developed signs of reverence such as kissing, incensing, bowing before, or lighting a vigil candle before an image. These gestures of reverence were sometimes misunderstood, not only by others, but also by the people giving the reverence, such that some may have been honoring the *objects* of art in themselves rather than for the *reminder* they provided of the saints. In the early eighth century came iconoclasm, a movement that decried the honoring of images, not only of saints, but also of God and angels. Iconoclasts saw superstition, idolatry, and magic in the veneration of images. Rather than just urging caution against excesses, they ruled out depicting figures on images entirely. Bloody persecutions of people who venerated images resulted because of this clash of views.

The Second Council of Nicaea in 787 supplied the Church's official rationale for the by-then-longstanding practice of honoring images. The council affirmed the then-already-known, and now classic, distinction between the adoration *(latreia)* due God alone, and the lesser honor of veneration *(dulia)* properly given to saints and angels. The council then went on to teach that images indeed may be honored, so long as the honor is directed not to the image in itself but beyond it to the one depicted.

90. What happened to the saints in art in the Middle Ages and afterward, down to recent times?

In the medieval period, many people experienced a definite distance from the sophistication of theology and of liturgies conducted in language and rituals they could not easily grasp. Into this gap came various popular devotions and accessible images. Artistic depictions of the saints were very helpful in this respect. This phenomenon points out an important principle from the study of religion: People need and want access to the divine and the holy, and they will try to get that in any way they can. Art became one of those possible ways.

Later in the Middle Ages, saints in art proliferated. Statues of saints began to be placed in town squares, at street corners, and along roads, usually in little shrines. The likenesses, which tended to

be homey and gentle, often won the hearts of passers-by and con-
tributed toward the phenomenon of people emulating saints. In general, the practice of depicting saints in art offered models of courage
against tough odds and also trust, not only in God's general care for
people, but also in God's power and mercy toward those needing the
attributes shown. As medieval devotion turned heavily toward won-
der-working saints, artists more frequently depicted saints as exer-
cising miraculous powers; for example, walking on water, healing
the sick, restoring the dead to life, or casting out demons.

Just before the Reformation era, depictions of any of a very
large number of saints made their way into homes, and small
paintings on wood grew numerous. Saints tended to be presented
individually, and with an air of calm dignity in place of themes of
violence and death.

After the Reformation, Catholic art of the saints took a turn
toward the simpler, the more didactic, and the more inspiring. As
Catholics asserted their teachings over against those rejected by
the Reformers, saints were drawn into art that stressed the
increasingly prominent themes of the conflict: for example, religious life, Eucharist, and mystical prayer. A favorite way of showing saints was to have them more or less at rest, in a pose the
Italians call *sacra conversazione,* not exactly conversation but
rather being together in a peaceful sharing. Mary is often in the
center of these pictures, and angels may frequently be present.

In later centuries, as missionary concerns were strong,
depictions of martyrs flourished as a way of instilling courage in
those bringing Christianity to new and strange lands. Then, in the
early nineteenth century, besides the art itself arose the science of
iconography, the study of the meaning of the art (not limited to
"icons") that religious people have fashioned and cherished
through the centuries.

Since the advent and popularity of photographs, the absolute
need for artistic conceptions of saints and symbols has lessened.
Occasionally, however, an artist will place a saint from recent centuries into an icon and include symbols that seem fitting to that saint.

91. Which saints are most frequently included in works of art?

By far, Mary is the most represented saint, and her visage is seen very frequently as the Madonna, the mother with the infant or child Jesus. Events in Christ's life, such as his birth, his moments of performing miracles, his Last Supper, and his death certainly account for much religious art. In these scenes Christ's closest disciples and Mary are often shown with him. There are also many illustrations of the Last Judgment and the life of heaven, and in these there are often victorious saints sharing in God's glory.

John the Baptist has often been rendered in art. He is almost always depicted wearing sheepskin and interacting with others. The Twelve (apostles) were among the first to be depicted as a group unto themselves. Then particular apostles were given physical characteristics that differentiated them and became quite standard. Paul was often portrayed with the apostles, frequently paired with Peter. The four evangelists were grouped together as well.

Other biblical saints figure prominently in events from Scripture. Some of the most notable are these: Joseph, often with Jesus and Mary, frequently depicted experiencing his dream or carrying his carpenter's tool; Martha, Mary, and Lazarus of Bethany; Mary Magdalen; and Old Testament figures such as Noah, Moses, Daniel, and Joseph.

Collected and individual saints belonging to the categories of martyrs, wonderworkers, founders of religious congregations, teachers, and charity-doers probably comprise the most captured saints in art.

92. Not all churches have images or statues of saints. Why?

Throughout the ages, many churches came to feature statues of saints. Almost every church contained at least a few, and a statue or other image of Mary became standard in most. Sometimes saints' images were quite close to the altar and tabernacle. Church buildings developed into centers not only for liturgy but also for personal devotion.

Vatican II's decree on liturgy *(Sacrosanctum Concilium)* called the Church back to a focus on the central theme of liturgy, the paschal mystery: the death and resurrection of Jesus Christ, carried out for the salvation of the whole world. Applying that "renewed" emphasis to matters of church art and furnishings, it follows that the altar or table (center of the Liturgy of the Eucharist), as well as the ambo or lectern (focus for the Liturgy of the Word), should be fairly prominent in every church. The tabernacle deserves its special place, too. So does the presider's chair, from which many of the prayers of the Mass are spoken. The architecture of any church must allow for the liturgy to be celebrated well. Celebrating the saints in the life of the Church is consistent with celebration of the paschal mystery, so their depictions are by no means forbidden. Still, they should not overpower. They must enter into the overall aim of the architecture of the church: not to detract but rather to enhance what happens. If fashioned and placed well, depictions of saints can enrich the liturgy. A church can indeed still be a place for personal prayer and devotion, such as to saints, but that use cannot become so prominent that the overall atmosphere of the church suffers.

Right after Vatican II, many churches reduced the number of depictions of saints, often out of a well-considered sense of giving greater attention to the Lord and to the paschal mystery celebrated in liturgy. In some of these, however, a certain starkness set in. In today's Church, there is room for differences in the way churches lead us to think about the things of God. But it is quite possible that, if we are not careful, some churches will have too few or too many depictions of saints, or they might not have them in good relation to the church's other furnishings.

93. Many people wanting to sell their houses have taken to burying a statue of St. Joseph in their yards. Is this practice advocated by the Church?

It is not. Though surely practiced and trusted by many, the custom smacks of a superstitious, mechanical approach to achieving a desired outcome without much involvement of the mind and heart; that is, without a real strong spirit of prayerfulness. Many who bury the statue would say that it needs to be placed upside down or that it has to be buried at night. It should be clear to people who understand the nature of real prayer that these features of the custom do not have much to do with faith, hope, and love. The custom puts too much emphasis on peripheral actions.

It is hard to know the origin of this tradition or the start of the association of St. Joseph with the intention of selling houses. It could well be that St. Joseph, head of the Holy Family, and patron of the universal Church, is a natural choice to be invoked for this need. Joseph is, after all, pictured often with Mary and Jesus in a home setting. Although this practice does show a respect for St. Joseph's being powerful, either as a direct bringer of a sale or as an intercessor whose prayers are heard and answered, it is not the best way to invoke St. Joseph. A simple, sincere prayer would be better. And yet all it takes for some people to continue the tradition is the news of a sale that seems linked to the action. For many, no amount of opposite reasoning will persuade them not to attempt it.

For those wanting to honor Joseph, a fuller, more God-centered devotion to him would be better. After all, Joseph is acclaimed principally as devoted foster-father of Jesus and chaste spouse of Mary. He is the "just man" (Matt 1:19) who shows faith in God's plan, obedience to God's will, respect for law, and bravery in crisis. His patronages are of the universal Church, those embracing celibate love, those who are dying, as well as workers and craftsmen.

EIGHT

SAINTS' NAMES AND REMAINS

94. What is the significance and background of the practice of giving or taking saints' names at baptism, and is it required?

The sixteenth-century *Catechism of the Council of Trent* taught the fittingness of this cherished custom. This opinion is still strong, although the practice less widespread. When that catechism was issued, most would have thought the custom originated in the time of the apostles. This is because St. John Chrysostom (347–407) criticized parents who went against what he termed a longstanding Christian practice. However, despite his words and occasional local decrees, evidence gleaned from earlier Christian writings and also from catacomb inscriptions shows that names of Christians in the first three centuries were little different from those of others. Names then tended to come from various inspirations, such as pagan mythology (e.g., Mercurius); numbers (Octavia); months (Januarius); personal qualities (Modestus); colors (Albanus); animals (Agnes); or agriculture (Agricia). As centuries passed, a good number of non-Christian names became saints' names because those bearing them were martyred or started to be honored as saints.

The rise of infant baptism naturally advanced the giving of Christian (including Old Testament and angels') names, since infants needed names anyhow. By the fourth century, with increased veneration of martyrs and biblical figures, Christians gradually became more likely to give their children saints' names.

Concerning the requirement, the 1917 *Code of Canon Law* decreed that a child being baptized be given a saint's name. At the baptism ceremony, if the parents had not chosen one, the law directed that the priest try to persuade them to do so. If he could not, then he was to add the name of a saint to the given one(s) and then insert also the saint's name in the official record book. Things changed in 1983, with promulgation of the new *Code of*

Canon Law. Its canon 855 states, "Parents, sponsors, and parish priests are to take care that a name is not given which is foreign to Christian sentiment." Thus, the requirement is gone now, although an awareness of the meaning of the name is implied.

Giving a saint's name obviously shows respect for saints, and it offers to the recipient the chance to have one or more saints as patrons, exemplars of the message that "Christian life can be well lived." Frequently a name that may not seem to be linked to a saint may indeed be. For instance, the girl's name Joann comes from the Latin version (Joannes) of the male name John. Carol derives from the Latin (Carolus) for the male Charles. Janet or Janice can be interpreted as a variation on Jane, a saint's name. While many children have been named for relatives or friends as much as for the saints themselves, the connection could still be made to the saint bearing that name. Many people holding a saint's name never know if their parents intended a particular saint; for example, which St. John or which St. Catherine.

If saints' names are to be influential, parents probably need to give some thought to the lives and virtues of the saints whose names they consider. Parents could expose their children to their name-saints' biographies and feast days. In some cultures a person's "name day" (usually their saint's feast) is an important day to celebrate, like or greater than a birthday.

95. And what is the significance of taking on an additional saint's name when being confirmed or joining a religious order?

For a long time, the custom of adding a new name of a saint to the baptismal name(s) was a prominent feature of the confirmation rite. This occurred during a long stretch when the close connection, indeed the continuity, between baptism and confirmation generally went understressed. In the rite revised after Vatican Council II, the candidate is simply "called by name." The confirmation recipient is not expected to have to choose a new name. In fact, the first name used since baptism is the one probably envisioned for the rite. In many dioceses and parishes, the older practice of adding a name is still allowed, however, with the result that some of those being confirmed, when called by name, hear a new name they themselves have selected. It is only reasonable that, if someone bothers to add a name, it should be a Christian one. For the growing number of Catholics being confirmed without ever having received a Christian name at baptism, the confirmation moment allows for selecting a saint's name with deliberation and a sense of why the saint behind the name can inspire a committed Christian life.

Until shortly after Vatican Council II, if someone entered most religious communities, a new Christian name was given to replace the baptismal name. The idea behind this name-changing practice was one of accentuating the change, the conversion of heart and mind, that religious life represented. In very many communities, one's family (last) name was not used in common address. Yet a few communities, even then, had members keep or merely supplement their baptismal name(s).

In response to Vatican II's emphasis on the universal call given by God through the Church for all to be holy from the moment of baptism onward, religious communities tend much more to retain baptismal names or perhaps to lengthen them with a new name. This retention communicates that living in consecrated life is a specification rather than a relinquishing of the way of life already lived since baptism. Some communities—more often the cloistered ones—still hold to the taking of a new name, but not for the purpose of denying or downplaying the deep holiness to which the baptized are called. In recent decades, the family name is more frequently heard and known than once was common, and this also hints at a similarity between lay and consecrated life in the Church.

96. What are relics of the saints, and what accounts for their notoriety?

Saints' relics include their dead bodies, often in small pieces (known as "real" or "first-class" relics), articles saints wore, used, or owned while on earth ("representative," "substitute," or "second-class" relics), and objects touched to these ("third-class" relics). The distinctly Christian meaning of the term has prevailed for centuries, but the Latin word *reliquiae* originally named any mortal remains.

Relics provide a link between the earthly and divine spheres of life. Main ways of honoring relics are praying close to them, kissing them, exposing them for honoring, carrying them in procession, visiting shrines holding them, and blessing people with them. A fixed altar should contain a relic. Relics became a mainstay of the veneration of the saints and of the devotional life of the Church in the Middle Ages, and Church authorities frequently needed to issue clarifications about them. The current *Code of Canon Law* (1983), in canon 1190, prohibits selling relics but not buying them. In fact, they *should* be purchased if that will remove them from situations of being disrespectfully kept. Fees can be charged in conveying a relic, so as to cover expenses.

Although the prominence of relics has declined over the past few centuries, the Church sees in them signs of the powerful presence of God splendidly alive in his saints. Arguments in support of relics' place in church life are probably much more persuasive for first-class than for other-class relics.

97. How did the honoring of saints' relics originate and then become such a mainstay?

Relic-veneration goes back to the honoring of martyrs, whose bones and possessions their fellow Christians kept and cherished. Both pagans and Christians generally respected the dead. While pagans frequently treated Christian martyrs as criminals and aimed to burn their bodies and scatter their ashes, fellow Christians loved them and so protected and prized their bodies.

Private honoring took a public turn early on, just after the martyrdom of Bishop Polycarp of Smyrna, who died at age eighty-six in the second century. His bones were esteemed as being more precious than gems or gold, and the Eucharist was celebrated at his burial place each year. Before long, there were reports of miracles resulting from praying near saints' relics.

In the fourth and fifth centuries, the practice of opening tombs of martyrs grew. Body parts or saints' buried objects were taken and divided for distribution. Enclosed in little cases (as many still are today), they were often worn around necks of devotees or placed in little private shrines. Relics frequently were kept in elaborate containers called reliquaries. Households, local church communities, towns, and religious confraternities and orders vied to own them, not only for their spiritual power but also for the prestige and influence that came to their owners.

In the early medieval period, some regional councils defended the importance of relics, but abuses in their use were condemned. A few centuries later, the Eastern practice of exhuming and dismembering bodies of saints became gradually acceptable in the West, and then the "translation" (moving) of relics to public shrines happened more and more. Larger relics were divided into smaller forms, and new ones were discovered. With all this activity came also the dissemination of many fraudulent relics. Economically, relics became important for fund-raising, as selling and exporting relics became big business!

The popularity of relics reached its height in the Middle Ages and particularly during the Crusades. Capturing relics and sacking relic collections happened primarily for their spiritual value. As they proliferated, however, individual relics decreased in value. In the late medieval period, it became regular practice that a consecrated altar contains relics of the patron saint (and this still holds). Many festivals of saints featured relics. Liturgical prayers were sparse in references to them, maybe because their inclusion in the altars in itself communicated how important they were.

98. What kinds of theological teaching and clarifications were needed in regard to relics, and in view of which problems?

Church leaders from the start do not seem to have obstructed the prizing, owning, and distributing of relics as incentives to remembering saints, praying to them, and being inspired by them. In time, prominent theologians of the fourth and fifth centuries, including doctors of the Church Basil the Great, John Chrysostom, Ambrose, and Augustine, affirmed the use of relics in devotion. The ongoing link between the dead and the living in the Body of Christ provided a theological foundation for the practice, as did the sense of respect for the body of those strong enough to die as martyrs and later as publicly acclaimed holy deceased. God's power and presence were thought to be localized in the saints when they were on earth, and there was a prevailing sense that God's ongoing life was somehow still at work through the relics. This sense was prone to be misunderstood or distorted into some kind of magic. So from nearly the start of the custom there were cautions or opposition.

Vigilantius saw use of relics as idolatrous, but his adversary St. Jerome (d. 419) defended use of them as in accord with Scripture and tradition, as well as instrumental in bringing about miracles. For him (as for many), relics were seen as efficacious: having the power to be conduits of God's grace to people. A contemporary of Jerome, Augustine, though convinced of the power of miracles associated with relics, showed disgust with people who sold counterfeit ones. In the East, St. John Damascene taught persuasively that relics were a gift from God for leading the Church to salvation and that the honoring of relics extended the honor owed only to God. This secured an already-strong sense of respect for relics in the East for many centuries afterwards.

Not surprisingly, problems loomed. One was superstition. Instead of being incentives to prayer and also reminders of the lives and virtues of saints, relics were for some people merely charms that owners carried or enshrined to bring good luck and to ward off evil. Another problem concerned what might be called the quantification of grace, counting up graces, as if to be stockpiled and used to insure salvation. There was—and can be in any age—a tendency to see salvation as brought about, not by how well one responds to God with faith, hope, and love (i.e., in a life of conversion and virtue), but rather by good external practices.

St. Bernard, in the twelfth century, expressed concern that relics detract from Christ, the supreme exemplar of the divine-human union. In the thirteenth century, Thomas Aquinas defended the veneration of relics but clarified again a teaching handed down from before: that the saints are the primary objects of veneration. The relics are but the sensible signs of God's power and love alive among the saints. A relic deserves honor but in a way not on a par with God nor with the relic's saint.

Two thirteenth-century Church councils at Lyons prohibited the honoring of new relics without papal approval. St. Thomas Aquinas, also in that century, taught that the relics of saints were the temples and instruments of the Holy Spirit's life in them when they were on earth. For him, since saints' relics are sure to be glorified at the resurrection of the body, they deserve respect.[27]

99. How did the Reformation critique play out with respect to relics?

Martin Luther (1483–1546) strongly criticized ownership of relics and especially reliance on them to achieve salvation. He saw them as lacking scriptural foundation and as being a ploy foisted on people by a Church looking to profit financially from trafficking in relics. However, Protestant reformer John Calvin spoke out against not relics in themselves but the abundance of relics whose authenticity could reasonably be questioned.

Catholic respondents pointed, as had others before them, to the instances in the Bible when people had touched Jesus' clothing and received healing; they saw in these encounters a basis for relics. The Council of Trent (held from 1545 to 1563), answering the objections raised by Reformers but also by concerned Catholics before and during the Reformation era, defended the

using and honoring of relics as consistent with the Church's tradition and long practice. Reasons were advanced in support of
relics: 1) saints' bodies are temples of the Holy Spirit; 2) saints,
with their bodies, are part of the Body of Christ; 3) the bodies of
saints, even in fragmentary pieces, are destined for the resurrection of the body; and 4) honor given to relics redounds to their
saints and Christ. In a nod to the existence of abuses, however, the
Council of Trent directed that no new relics should be made man-
ifest in a diocese without the diocesan bishop's approval of them.
This same council set in place the prohibition of selling relics.

100. Who are the "incorruptibles"?

The term *incorruptibles* refers to certain saints and potential
saints whose bodies apparently have not undergone the normal
processes of decomposition even though they have not been
deliberately or accidentally preserved. Factors that would contribute to deliberate or accidental preservation include hermetic
sealing (exclusion of air) and freedom from bacteria. Yet even
excluding these bodies, as well as any that might be proven
hoaxes, there are still enough genuine and totally unexplained incorruptibles that its occurrence can be held real.

A sense of mystery surrounds this phenomenon. Claims that
some particular saints' bodies have remained incorrupt have been
made from the first century through the present, and the evidence
continues to amaze people and baffle scientists. For many incorruptibles, their bodies were exposed, it seems, not only to conditions that would make for the usual decomposition; but also, prior
to death, to disease or violence that would normally weaken the
bodies further.

Signs of incorruptibility, not all of them always present,
include the absence of rigor mortis and of dryness (which differen-
tiates the typically flexible and "moist" incorruptibles from natural
mummies), the emanation of a pleasant fragrance, and the exuda-
tion of oil. More rarely made are claims of continued bleeding long

after death, warmth well after death, and spontaneous random movement of parts long after death. Sometimes, just a part of a body remains free of decomposition.

Sometimes efforts have been made to help a body decompose, and still resistance has occurred. Lime, a decaying agent, could not do its usual work with the bodies of Sts. Francis Xavier, John of the Cross, and Paschal Baylon, all from the sixteenth century.

101. What religious interpretation has been given to this phenomenon?

For centuries, many have advanced it as God's indicating the holiness of the saints. Many would see incorruptibility as pointing to Christ's own victory over death and as affirming the Catholic belief in the resurrection of the body.

In the Middle Ages, churches that displayed saints' incorruptible bodies became popular for prayer and pilgrimage. The bodies of candidates for canonized sainthood often were exhumed so that incorruptibility could be determined. Many witnesses customarily attested to those findings.

As with any extraordinary happenings centered on religious matters, reserve ought to be exercised, and presumably has been, lest frauds and "wishful thinking" cloud the serious investigation of a specific body's state. Obviously, some cautionary words have to be kept in mind. First of all, sanctity does not depend on this or any other extraordinary phenomena; these are not a sure sign of holiness. Second, many saints have bodies that have corrupted in the normal way. Third, a body could be incorrupt without one's being considered a saint, and indeed in many places and instances bodies have remained more or less intact without the suggestion of outstanding Christian holiness. The phenomenon cuts across cultures and religions, and many bodies of those outside Catholicism and Christianity have been considered incorrupt. There may be even more than we know, since comparatively few "nonsaints" have had their bodies disinterred for examination as have candidates for canonized sainthood.

NOTES

1. I am indebted to Elizabeth A. Johnson for her early article "Communion of Saints: Partners on the Way," *Church* 5 (Summer 1989): 17–21, with its clear presentation of the image of the circle, explained more fully than I have here. In addition, the idea of Christ's being at the center and of people growing in closeness to one another as they draw nearer to Christ depends on the imagination of Dorotheus of Gaza, whose ideas about God at the center are quoted and explained in Roberta C. Bondi, *To Love as God Loves: Conversations with the Early Church* (Philadelphia: Fortress Press, 1987), 24–25; and in Elizabeth A. Johnson, *Friends of God and Prophets: A Feminist Theological Reading of the Communion of Saints* (New York: Continuum, 1998), 14–15.

2. In this vein, see Avery Dulles, *The Catholicity of the Church* (Oxford: Clarendon Press, 1985), 5–8, for his brief exposition and creative adaptation of two of Paul Tillich's ideas of the "Catholic substance" of Christianity and the "Protestant principle," as well as of Carl J. Peter's proposal of a related "Catholic principle."

3. William G. Thompson, SJ, "Spirituality, Spiritual Development, and Holiness," *Review for Religious* 51 (1992): 654–55.

4. Peter Brown, "The Rise and Function of the Holy Man in Late Antiquity," *The Journal of Roman Studies* 61 (1971): 80–101.

5. Lawrence Cunningham, *The Catholic Heritage* (New York: Crossroad, 1983). These are some of the classifications that provide the chapter titles of this book.

6. Johnson, *Friends of God and Prophets,* 8.

7. Robert A. Orsi's *Thank You, Saint Jude: Women's Devotion to the Patron Saint of Hopeless Causes* (New Haven, CT: Yale University Press, 1996) provides a full study of the twentieth-century cult of St. Jude.

8. The Smalcald Articles in *The Book of Concord: The Confessions of the Evangelical Lutheran Church,* trans. and ed. Theodore G. Tappert (Philadelphia: Fortress, 1959), 297.

9. *The Martyrdom of St. Polycarp* in Ancient Christian Writers series, vol. 6 (New York: Newman Press, 1948), 9:3.

10. St. Augustine, "Letter to Festus" (Letter 89) pp. 34–40, Fathers of the Church series, vol 18 (Washington, DC: The Catholic University of America Press, 1953), p. 35.

11. St. Thomas Aquinas, *Summa Theologiae,* II–II, q. 124, a. 5.

12. Richard M. Peterson, "Hagiography," *Westminster Dictionary of Christian Spirituality,* ed. Gordon S. Wakefield (Philadelphia: The Westminster Press, 1983).

13. Sherry L. Reames, *The Legenda Aurea: A Reexamination of Its Paradoxical History* (Madison: University of Wisconsin Press, 1985).

14. Hippolyte Delehaye, *The Legends of the Saints* (London: Geoffrey Chapman, 1962), 170–81.

15. *Sacrosanctum Concilium, #92.*

16. Dan Brown, *The Da Vinci Code* (New York: Random House, 2003).

17. James Wallace, *Preaching through the Saints* (Collegeville, MN: Liturgical Press, 1982), 36–42.

18. Ibid., 31.

19. Ibid., 38.

20. Ibid.

21. Ibid., 31–32.

22. Ibid., 41.

23. *Sacrosanctum Concilium, #108.*

24. Ibid., #106.

25. Ibid., #111.

26. Concilium for the Implementation of the Constitution on the Sacred Liturgy, "Commentary on the General Norms for the Liturgical Year and the Calendar" (1969), published in *Norms Governing Liturgical Calendars* (Washington, DC: United States Catholic Conference, 1984), 72.

27. St. Thomas Aquinas, *Summa Theologiae,* III, q. 25, a. 6.